SUFFOLK RECORDS SOCIETY

SUFFOLK CHARTERS

Founding Editor
the late R. Allen Brown

XVII

THE PAKENHAM CARTULARY FOR THE MANOR OF IXWORTH THORPE, SUFFOLK c.1250–c.1320

The Pakenham cartulary for the manor of Ixworth Thorpe in Suffolk is one of the few secular medieval cartularies to survive. It is especially deserving of attention for its demonstration of the importance families of the Pakenham class attached to the provision of inheritances for their younger sons. Thomas of Pakenham, the man for whom the cartulary was composed, was the second son of the knight Sir William of Pakenham; his elder brother Edmund was the main beneficiary of their father's estate, but it is clear that Sir William wished to provide for all his sons: the manor of Ixworth Thorpe was Thomas's inheritance. The charters collected in this cartulary represent the assets of Sir William in the vill, accumulated over a period of about fifty years, plus acquisitions made by Thomas after his father's death.

Dr S. D. CHURCH is Senior Lecturer in History, University of East Anglia.

SUFFOLK RECORDS SOCIETY

SUFFOLK CHARTERS

ISSN 0261–9938

General Editor
Professor Christopher Harper-Bill

Details of previously published volumes of Suffolk Charters
are available from the publishers

THE PAKENHAM CARTULARY FOR THE MANOR OF IXWORTH THORPE, SUFFOLK c.1250–c.1320

Edited by S. D. Church

The Boydell Press

Suffolk Records Society

First published 2001

Published for the Suffolk Records Society
by The Boydell Press
an imprint of Boydell & Brewer Ltd
PO Box 9, Woodbridge, Suffolk IP12 3DF, UK
and of Boydell & Brewer Inc.
PO Box 41026, Rochester, NY 14604–4126, USA
website: http://www.boydell.co.uk

ISBN 0 85115 835 8

A catalogue record for this book is available
from the British Library

This publication is printed on acid-free paper

Printed in Great Britain by
Antony Rowe Ltd, Chippenham, Wiltshire

CONTENTS

ILLUSTRATIONS

To Maria Sophia Quine and Samuel Church

This volume is published with the assistance of
a grant from Isobel Thornley's Bequest to
the University of London

PREFACE

In the production of this volume I have incurred innumerable debts, the most important of which is to my friend, colleague and the general editor of this series, Professor Christopher Harper-Bill. When he gave me this cartulary to edit (rather longer ago than either he or I would like to remember), he said it would 'do me good'. I am happy to report that he was right. He has also provided an invaluable service as general editor, invariably picking up my infelicities and smoothing out the rough edges in my calendar. Vivien Brown, with much profit to me, has also cast her eye over this calendar, and to her I also offer my gratitude. I would also like to record my thanks to the following scholars: Miss Susan Reynolds and Dr Ann Williams, who supported me in the completion of this project; Dr Robert Liddiard, who put at my disposal his knowledge of landscape archaeology; Dr Paul Brand and Mrs Elizabeth Rutledge, who gave me advice on the mysteries of medieval conveyancing; Dr Michelle Brown, who helped me decipher an inscription in the cartulary; Dr Mark Bailey, who shared his insights into the economy of medieval East Anglia; Philip Judge, who expertly turned my scribbles into readable maps; Dr Chris Lewis, Dr Tom Williamson, and Dr Carole Rawcliffe, who extended various kindnesses; and Mr John Cross, who allowed me to tramp across his land and gave me access to two maps of Ixworth in his possession. I would also like to put on record my thanks to the burgeoning community of postgraduates in medieval history at East Anglia; they tolerated my silly questions on various aspects of late medieval history. More generally, the staffs at the Suffolk Record Office, Bury St Edmunds, The British Library and the Cambridge University Library have, by their generosity, also aided greatly the preparation of this calendar. In addition I have received financial support from the Arts and Humanities Research Board, which funded a semester's study leave, from the Isobel Thornley Bequest, which provided some funds towards the publication costs of this volume, and from my own institution, the University of East Anglia, which gave me study leave in the academic year 1999–2000. But despite all the expert help that I have had at my disposal in the preparation of this calendar, errors remain. These errors are my own, carelessly crafted in the confines of my home and rendered here in print to confuse and confound posterity.

From the footnotes and the material collected in the section labelled 'Biographical List', it will be abundantly clear that I owe a great scholarly debt to Edgar Powell. His extraordinarily useful *A Suffolk Hundred in the Year 1283* (Cambridge 1910) was my constant companion while writing the introduction and dating the undated charters. The work (an edition of a 1280 return compiled for St Edmunds in the 1330s and a tabulated version of the tax return for the subsidy of 1283) covers, happily for me, Blackbourn hundred, the hundred in which Ixworth Thorpe lies. Without his work, this particular contribution to the history of medieval Suffolk would have been much the poorer.

This volume is dedicated to my wife, Dr Maria Sophia Quine, and my son, Samuel Church, each of whom has contributed to the maintenance of my sanity in the strange world of late thirteenth- and early fourteenth-century local society – a place where, having been reared in the aristocratic and royal worlds of the Old English, Norman and Angevin past, I still feel very ill-at-ease.

Norwich
The Feast of St Michael 2000

ABBREVIATIONS

AgHR	*Agricultural History Review*
Book of Fees	*Liber Feodorum: the Book of Fees commonly called Testa de Nevill*, ed. H.C. Maxwell-Lyte, 3 vols, London 1920–31
BL	British Library
Bloomfield, *Norfolk*	F. Bloomfield and C. Parkin, *An Essay towards a Topographical History of Norfolk*, 11 vols, London 1805–10
Ca.	Cambridgeshire
Cal. Charter Rolls	*Calendar of Charter Rolls*, 6 vols, London 1902 etc.
Cal. Close Rolls	*Calendar of Close Rolls*, 67 vols, London 1903 etc.
Cal. Fine Rolls	*Calendar of Fine Rolls*, 21 vols, London 1911 etc.
Cal. Genealogicum	*Calendarium Genealogicum Henry III and Edward I*, 2 vols, ed. C. Roberts, London 1865
Cal. Patent Rolls	*Calendar of Patent Rolls*, 60 vols, London 1901 etc.
CIPM	*Calendar of Inquisitions Post Mortem*, 16 vols, London 1917 etc.
Copinger, *Manors*	W.A. Copinger, *Manors of Suffolk: Notes on their History and Devolution*, 7 vols, London 1905–11
Copinger, *Materials*	W.A. Copinger, *Materials for the History of Suffolk*, 6 vols, London 1904–7
CUL	Cambridge University Library
EcHR	*Economic History Review*
Ex. Rot. Fin.	*Excerpta e Rotulis Finum*, ed. C. Roberts, 2 vols, Record Commission, London 1835–6
Feudal Aids	*Inquisitions and Assessments relating to Feudal Aids AD 1284–1431*, 6 vols, London 1899–1908
kt	Knight
LDB	*Little Domesday Book*
Li.	Lincolnshire
Mr	*Magister*
Monasticon	*Monasticon Anglicanum* of William Dugdale, ed. J. Caley *et al.*, 6 vols in 8 parts, London 1817–30
Nf.	Norfolk
OSA	Order of St Augustine
OSB	Order of St Benedict
Pinchbeck	F. Hervey, ed., *The Pinchbeck Register*, 2 vols, Brighton 1925
Placitorum	*Placitorum in Domo Capitulari Westmonasteriensi asservatorum Abbreviatio* (Rich I–Edw II), ed. W. Illingworth, Record Commission, London 1811

Rot. Hund.	*Rotuli Hundredorum temp. Henry III et Edward I*, ed. W. Illingworth, 2 vols, Record Commission, London 1812–18
Rye, *FF Norfolk*	W. Rye, *A Short Calendar of the Feet of Fines for Norfolk in the Reigns of Richard I, John, Henry III and Edward I*, Norwich 1888
Rye, *FF Suffolk*	W. Rye, *A Calendar of the Feet of Fines for Suffolk*, Ipswich 1900
Som.	Somerset
State Trials	*State Trials of the Reign of Edward the First, 1289–1293*, ed. T.F. Tout and H. Johnstone, Camden 3rd series, 9, 1906
Suffolk Hundred	*A Suffolk Hundred in the Year 1283*, ed. E. Powell, Cambridge 1910
SRO	Suffolk Record Office
t./tt.	table/tables
unid.	unidentified
Valor Ecclesiasticus	*Valor Ecclesiasticus*, ed. J. Caley and J. Hunter, 6 vols, Record Commission, London 1810 etc.
VCH	*Victoria County History*
Wlt	Wiltshire
Wt	Isle of Wight

CHRONOLOGICAL LIST OF CHARTERS

CONCORDANCE OF MANUSCRIPT CHARTERS WITH THIS EDITION

Nos in this edn	*Nos in MS*	*Folio no.*
1–89	1–89	1r–16v
90	90	16v–21r
91	119	21r
92	120	
93	121	
94	122	21v
95	123	
96	124	
97	125	22r
98	126	
99	127	
100	128	
101	129	22v
102	130	
103	131	
104	132	23r
105	133	
106	134	
107	135	23v
108	136	
109	137	
110	138	
111	139	24r
112	140	
113	141	24v
114	142	
115	143	
116	91	17r
117	92	
118	93	
119	94	17v
120	95	
121	96	
122	97	
123	98	18r
124	99	
125	100	
126	101	18v
127	102	
128	103	
129	104	
130	105	19r
131	106	
132	107	
133	108	
134	109	19v
135	110	
136	111	
137	112	
138	113	20r
137	114	
140	115	
141	116	20v
142	117	
143	118	
144–78	144–78	25r–31r

INTRODUCTION

In the autumn of 1304, Sir William of Pakenham, knight, began to make disposition of his property to his sons. Sir William's eldest son, Edmund of Pakenham, was to succeed his father in the majority of his lands, but it is clear that Sir William also wished to provide for his other two sons, Thomas and William. With this aim in mind, at the important Pakenham manor of Norton on 6 October 1304, William son of Sir William of Pakenham quitclaimed to his father for himself and his heirs all rights that he had in the manor of Ixworth Thorpe (5). One month later, after Sir William's death, though presumably at his instigation, and also at the manor of Norton, Edmund of Pakenham granted to his brother Thomas the whole manor of Ixworth Thorpe in heredity to be held of Edmund and his heirs, saving a certain fishery that their father had bought from William de Criketot,[1] with reversion to Edmund's line should Thomas die without legal issue. For this grant Thomas paid the princely sum of 100 marks in cash (6). That same day Edmund wrote to his free tenants and others belonging to the manor of Ixworth Thorpe mandating them to submit and answer to Thomas for the manor (131). With these actions, in the case of Thomas, Sir William of Pakenham's wishes had been fulfilled, and Thomas was able to use the manor of Ixworth Thorpe to support himself and his family.

Ixworth Thorpe was not Sir William of Pakenham's only manor; in fact it made up only a portion of a much larger holding centred on Suffolk but with outposts in Norfolk and even further afield. At Norton in Blackbourn hundred Sir William held land assessed at ¾ of a knight's fee.[2] Although it is not apparent how much land this comprised, we might reasonably suppose that it was a sizeable manor. In 1283, for example, when Edward I sent his commissioners into the country to assess the value of movables from which he had been granted a thirtieth to fund his campaign in Wales, Sir William's assessment in the vill of Norton amounted to £38 1s 0d.[3] At Ixworth Thorpe, the assessment for the purposes of the 1283 tax was £34 3s 5¼d and this was on land measured at 120 acres or more along with a manor house.[4] Presumably Sir William's holding at Norton was significant. At Bardwell, too, Sir William must have held considerable amounts of property since his assessment in this vill in 1283 was £26 15s 6d. The landholding here was later assessed at ¼ of a knight's fee.[5] And finally in

1 The significance of this reservation is discussed below on pp. 5–6.

2 *Feudal Aids*, v, 72.

3 *Suffolk Hundred*, t. 23.

4 *Suffolk Hundred*, t. 31; 44.

5 *Suffolk Hundred*, t. 3; *Feudal Aids*, v, 72.

Blackbourn hundred, Sir William held movables in Great Ashfield assessed at £9 12s 6d.[6]

Sir William's other major estate centres were in Thedwastre hundred. Here we are fortunate in that the returns as to landholding made by Solomon of Rochester for Edward I in 1280 and copied by a Bury scribe in the 1330s have survived to give us a detailed account of the lands that Sir William held of the abbot and convent.[7] In the vill of Thurston, Sir William held 240 acres from the abbot of St Edmunds owing service of a ¼ of a knight's fee plus another 6 acres with suit to the hundred and another 33 acres of Richard Claviger; in addition he had 20 acres of land in the hands of his villeins and another 43½ acres of land held by his tenants with sundry messuages.[8] Another centre of Sir William's landholding was at Pakenham, the place from which the family presumably took its name. Here he held 56 acres of land and 4 acres of meadow of the convent of St Edmunds; in addition he had 42 acres of land in the hands of his villeins and a further 304 acres and a rood of land, 12½ acres of meadow and a mill in the hands of his tenants with their messuages.[9] Sir William also had interests in Chevington (Thingoe hundred), Ampton (Thedwastre), and Barton (Thedwastre) totalling 165 acres of land plus meadowland and woodland.[10] And he had minor interests in Sharneburn, Norfolk[11] and in Merstone, Isle of Wight.[12]

It must be presumed that the major source of Sir William's income came from the land. According to the tax list of 1283, in Blackbourn hundred alone Sir William's movables were assessed at £108 12s 6d.[13] This assessment included three of Sir William's major manors of Norton, Ixworth Thorpe and Bardwell and the important manor of Great Ashfield, but it did not include the two other major manors of Pakenham and Thurston, and nor did it include Sir William's other manors in Suffolk and elsewhere. Were the assessment of Sir William's other lands to have survived, we should not be surprised to see his movables assessed at in excess of £200. In the assessment of 1283, moreover, there were a number of important exclusions from the tax including 'treasure, riding horses, bedding, clothes, vessels, tools, geese, capons, hens, bread, wine, ale, cider' and anything that was destined for consumption by the household.[14] And furthermore, it is now widely accepted that there was a considerable amount of under-assessment going

6 *Suffolk Hundred*, 76. In addition Sir William held 3 acres at Stowlangtoft and 3 acres at Stanton (*Suffolk Hundred*, 17, 49).

7 The account for Blackbourn hundred, which includes Ixworth Thorpe, but not the other manors in which Sir William was a major landholder, was printed by Edgar Powell in his *Suffolk Hundred*, 1–65. The hundreds of Hertismere, Babergh, Thedwastre, Thingoe, Lackford, Cosford, and Risbridge, along with Blackbourn hundred, are printed in Lord Francis Hervey's *Pinchbeck*, ii, 30–282.

8 *Pinchbeck*, ii, 138–9; *Feudal Aids*, v, 30, 75.

9 *Pinchbeck*, ii, 140–1; the family's interests in the vill can be traced back to a John son of John of Pakenham at the time of Abbot Simon of Luton (1257–79) (*Pinchbeck*, i, 465–7).

10 *Pinchbeck*, ii, 106, 122–3, 156.

11 *Feudal Aids*, iii, 449, 523; *CIPM*, iv, nn. 293, 391 (261); *Cal. Fine Rolls*, i, 523, 528; *Cal. Close Rolls, 1307–13*, 100; *Placitorum*, 321 b.

12 *Cal. Fine Rolls*, i, 513.

13 *Suffolk Hundred*, xx.

14 J.F. Willard, *Parliamentary Taxes on Personal Property 1290–1334*, Cambridge, Mass., 1934, 84.

on in these returns.[15] The assessors worked by a set of 'standard prices' agreeable to all parties involved and usually set at the lower end of the market value. They also tended to under-report the quantities of movables to be assessed. It has been observed, for example, that 'few communities could subsist on the food supplies valued for the subsidies' and it is clear that when it is possible to compare tax returns with other, non tax-related documents, assessors also under reported the amount of livestock on the land. In short, like all communities subject to tax, the men and women of Suffolk did their best to minimise its impact. In this context Sir William of Pakenham appears as a very rich man indeed, especially when his movables are seen in the light of the various distraints on knighthood issued by Edward I. In 1285, for example, the king decreed that only those holding £100 of land should be required to assume the obligations of knighthood;[16] Sir William would very easily have fitted into this category.

Ixworth Thorpe

The Pakenham property at Ixworth Thorpe seems to have originally comprised three parcels coming from two distinct sources. The first two parcels originally constituted two holdings of the Blund family dating from the time of Abbot Baldwin (1065–97). It was the tradition at St Edmunds that at this time Robert le Blund was enfeoffed by the abbot with two moieties of 60 acres each at Ixworth Thorpe along with a church with 12 acres of land attached.[17] By the time of Abbot Samson (1182–1211), this land, for which the holder William le Blund owed the service of a knight, was in the custody of Brian fitz Ralph.[18] Long before 1259, the land at Ixworth Thorpe was granted to Mr John of Pakenham who held it of the Blund family.[19] Sometime before 12 May 1259, he in his turn granted in heredity to Sir William and Sir William's brother John of Pakenham to hold of himself and his heirs all his lands and tenements in Ixworth Thorpe in return for an annuity of £40 payable in two equal instalments at Michaelmas and at Easter (4). According to the Bury copy of the 1280 return, Sir William was the capital lord of the vill holding a messuage, 120 acres of arable land, 5 acres of meadow, an acre of wood, 1½ acres of pasture and a warren for which he owed service for a knight's fee and services to the ward of Norwich castle and to the sheriff. He held this of the heirs of Mr John of Pakenham who held of the heirs of William le Blund who held of the abbot of St Edmunds who held of the king in chief.[20]

The second distinct source of Sir William of Pakenham's land at Ixworth

15 For what follows see J.F. Hadwin, 'The medieval lay subsidies and economic history', *EcHR*, 2nd ser., 36 (1983), 200–17.

16 F.M. Powicke, *The Thirteenth Century, 1216–1307*, Oxford 1953, 545–54 (at 552).

17 *Pinchbeck*, i, 420; confirmed, though without mention of the church, by *LDB*, fo. 367b.

18 *Pinchbeck*, i, 330–1. There was another knight's fee at Ixworth Thorpe during this time that was in the hands of Roger de Morieux, though after he relinquished the property it fell into the hands of the abbot of Bury (*Pinchbeck*, i, 284–5).

19 *Book of Fees*, 601; *Pinchbeck*, i, 277.

20 *Suffolk Hundred*, 44.

Thorpe was the family of Geoffrey of Thorpe. This land was assessed at ½ a knight's fee and in 1236 was in the Valoignes barony and was held by Margaret de Rivers along with a knight's fee at Little Fakenham and a ¼ of a knight's fee at Sapiston.[21] By 1242–3, Ixworth Thorpe and Little Fakenham were in the hands of David Cumyn.[22] From him in a way that is as yet unfathomable, the land passed to Geoffrey of Thorpe who before 1263 began to enfeoff Sir William with the land.[23] This land in Ixworth Thorpe was not held of St Edmunds, hence it does not appear in the abbey's copy of the return of 1280.[24]

There were three other discrete pieces of land at Ixworth Thorpe recorded in the pages of Little Domesday besides the three pieces already mentioned. The first, held of the abbey of St Edmunds, was in 1086 held by two freemen.[25] It is not unreasonable to suppose that the two holders of the abbot's lands mentioned in the abbey's copy of the 1280 return were successors of the two freemen mentioned in Domesday. William le Sire held 3 acres of the abbot for 3d a year and Robert Puttock held a messuage, 2 acres of arable land and 5 roods of meadow for 4d a year.[26] And interestingly, too, given his surname, Robert Puttock (*Puttoc*, OE kite)[27] may have been a direct descendant of one of the freemen Domesday mentions but does not name. Of the descent of the second and third pieces of land mentioned in Domesday, little is known.[28] It is worth pointing out, however, that the land held by the otherwise obscure Sasselin was held as a manor by his pre-Conquest antecessor, Acwulf. Moreover, William de Criketot was said to hold in chief in the vill in the fourteenth century and so was presumably holding this manor.[29]

The means by which Sir William consolidated his hold over the manor of Ixworth Thorpe are amply demonstrated by the series of charters preserved in this cartulary. Until the charters of Sir William's son Thomas, the practice was, in most cases, to give the purchase price in the text of the deed. The documents show that Sir William spent a considerable amount of money in building up his

21 *Book of Fees*, 579; this is presumably the 30 acres held by Sparrowhawk of Peter de Valoignes recorded in *LDB*, fo. 421a.

22 *Book of Fees*, 919.

23 *Pinchbeck*, i, 276.

24 Which serves to remind us of the important point that this survey as it survives to us includes only those lands in which the abbot and/or convent had an interest. It does not give a total picture of land tenure in a particular vill as is illustrated by the fact that in this instance the lands acquired from Geoffrey of Thorpe receive no mention. The scribe or scribes who in the 1330s copied out the relevant entries for the abbot and convent from the 1280 return were also not averse to abbreviating the entries. Under Ixworth Thorpe and Sir William's entry, for example, the scribe has copied slavishly the comment that Sir William owes a knight's fee 'pro se et tenentibus suis subscriptis'. In this instance, however, Sir William's tenants have been omitted. It is worth noting, however, that in the early fourteenth century at St Edmunds there was a notion that Sir William owed service for two separate pieces of one knight's fee and half a knight's fee (BL Harleian MS 230, fos 67r, 67v; BL Harleian MS 743, fos 125v, 125v–126r).

25 *LDB*, fo. 367a.

26 *Suffolk Hundred*, 44.

27 *A Thesaurus of Old English*, 2 vols, ed. J. Roberts, C. Kay with L. Grundy, King's College London Centre for Late Antique and Medieval Studies, London 1995, i, 92.

28 *LDB*, fos 436b, 447a.

29 *Feudal Aids*, 46.

estate at Ixworth Thorpe. The grant from Mr John of Pakenham alone was to cost Sir William and his brother John £40 p.a. during their uncle's lifetime and then after his death £20 p.a. to his heirs (4). In addition to this annual outlay, Sir William paid out in excess of £140 for the lands he acquired in Ixworth Thorpe.[30]

Once Thomas of Pakenham had entered into his inheritance at Ixworth Thorpe, he, like his father, though without the financial resources that his father could deploy, continued the task of consolidating his hold over the manor. Unfortunately, because of a change in diplomatic practice, the charters of Thomas do not record the amounts of money he paid to obtain the grants that are here recorded.[31] It is not possible, therefore, to calculate how much money Thomas spent on his acquisitions. What is noticeable, however, is that although there are fewer acts recorded for Thomas, he entered into more exchanges with other landholders in the manor than had his father. There are nine exchanges recorded for Thomas, five of which were made with William Kenne (148, 158, 170, 173, 174), with whom Thomas seems to have had a disagreement that was eventually resolved in June 1319 (173). The remaining four exchanges were made with four separate residents of Ixworth Thorpe (152, 153, 154, 155). Thomas does seem to have spent time and money consolidating his hold over the manor. His purchases, though, consisted mostly of meadowland, and these small quantities, perhaps reflecting the fact that his father had done the donkey work in creating the holding at Ixworth Thorpe.

It is certain that Sir William was determined to pass onto Thomas Ixworth Thorpe; the quitclaim by Sir William's son William makes that clear (5). But Sir William did not himself grant that land to Thomas; rather he left it for his eldest son and heir Edmund to do that (6). Two key economic assets and social indicators, however, were retained in Edmund's hands. The first was the fishery that Sir William had bought from William de Criketot. Was that reservation part of Sir William's plan or did Edmund act on his own initiative? Of course, we shall never know the answer to that question. The second asset that Edmund retained was that of free warren in Ixworth Thorpe. As we have seen, this privilege had been granted to Sir William in 1259 and again in 1292 when it was extended to his other major manors.[32] The important point to note about grants of free warren is that they did not attach simply to land, rather they were granted to specific individuals and their heirs to be exercised in named places. The heir to the warren (or possibly warrens, given the existence of the second grant) in Ixworth Thorpe was Edmund of Pakenham, not his brother Thomas, and it seems that Edmund retained this asset, too. Although there is no mention of the warren in the cartulary, in June 1318, Thomas of Pakenham was granted free warren in Ixworth Thorpe, 'on the information of Mr Thomas of Charlton'.[33] Whether this grant represented a new warren or related to the warren that must have been in Edmund's hands remains unclear. What does seem certain is that for at least thir-

30 The total recorded in the charters printed here is £137 17s, but this underestimates the total cost, since a number of the charters do not record the purchase price.

31 The new formula is 'for a certain sum of money which he/they gave in cash'.

32 *Cal. Charter Rolls, 1257–1300*, 17, 422.

33 *Cal. Charter Rolls, 1300–26*, 382.

teen years, Edmund of Pakenham retained major economic assets in the manor.[34] This must have been a source of much irritation to Thomas. Fishing rights and rights of warren were economically important, to be sure, but they were also key social indicators. By retaining fishing rights and the right of warren, Edmund was constantly reminding his younger brother that he, not Thomas, was the true lord of the manor.

Towards the end of his life, Thomas of Pakenham, just as his father had done for him, began to make provision for his children's inheritances. The manor itself was to descend to Thomas and Alice's first son, Theobald, though even before that event Thomas and Alice made provision for his inheritance of some land in the manor (165). Rose, their daughter, got a piece of arable land (167) for her lifetime and William, their second son, got two messuages, 56 acres of land, 2½ acres of meadow and rents worth 5s for his lifetime (168, 169, cf. 169a).

After Theobald's death, the manor descended to Theobald's son, John of Pakenham.[35] John married Agnes daughter of Thomas of Saxham and their daughter and heir, Margaret, married William of Bardwell (d. 1434).[36] Having bought out his widowed mother-in-law's share of Ixworth Thorpe in October 1395,[37] in July 1403, William, with Margaret, sold a number of their manors including Ixworth Thorpe to Roger Drury, Nicholas Rys, Nicholas Drury, John Lodewyn, Thomas Sarre and Robert Grandesdene.[38] At some point in the fifteenth century, the manor came into the possession of Ixworth priory, where it remained until the dissolution.[39]

Ixworth Thorpe: A Topographical Discussion

As we have seen, at the time of Domesday there were two distinct manors in Ixworth Thorpe. The first, held by Robert le Blund of the abbot of St Edmunds,[40] was to become the centre of William of Pakenham's holding in the vill; Sasselin held the second in chief of the king.[41] Field walking in the area has shown that there appears to have been two foci of settlement in the medieval period,[42] and presumably these represent the two manors we know to have existed at this time. The first of these is clustered around the common at the north end of the parish and remains today as the site of the modern village of Ixworth Thorpe. The second settlement appears to have been at the southern edge of the parish around

34 M. Bailey, 'The rabbit and the medieval East Anglian economy', *AgHR*, 36 (1988), 1–20; C.K. Currie, 'The early history of the carp and its economic significance in England', *AgHR*, 39 (1991), 97–107.

35 *Feudal Aids*, v, 72.

36 Copinger, *Manors*, i, 380–1.

37 BL Harleian Charter, 54 F 7.

38 BL Additional Charter 15537.

39 Copinger, *Manors*, i, 380–1; *Valor Ecclesiasticus*, iii, 482.

40 *LDB*, fo. 420b.

41 *LDB*, fo. 436b.

42 E. Savery, A. Smith, E. Martin, 'Ixworth Thorpe', in *Medieval Settlement Research Group Annual Report*, 8 (1993), 50–1. This article neatly summarises the field-walking evidence.

a green, part of which is marked on a map of 1725 as 'inter common'.[43] This settlement was presumably associated with a house whose existence was preserved in the eighteenth century by the field-name 'Thorpe Hall'. There is certainly evidence that there was some sort of building located here, though it had long gone by 1725.[44]

The charters preserved in the cartulary and calendared here show that the Pakenham holding was a typical medieval manor. The overwhelming impression is of irregular open field cultivation with strips of land located within furlongs, as is attested by the frequent mention of headlands in the charters, and with numbers of furlongs located within in large open fields.[45] Map 2 attempts to show the location of some of the features that would have been apparent in the fourteenth century. The material has been taken from the two maps dating from the eighteenth century.[46] Despite the fact that these maps are late and record a landscape that had been enclosed by the time that they were drawn, they do give us some useful indication of the type of land use we might expect to have seen in the fourteenth century. It is likely, for example, that the heathland recorded in the eighteenth century would have been in the same location in the fourteenth century, even if then its extent had been greater. Equally it is certain that the land recorded as pasture and meadow in the eighteenth century performed a similar function in the fourteenth. It has seemed reasonable, therefore, to indicate the likely areas of heath, meadow and pasture from the eighteenth-century evidence.

Although the field boundaries changed in the five centuries between the Ixworth Thorpe known to Sir William of Pakenham and his son and that shown by the maps of 1725 and 1769, the eighteenth-century field-names have preserved a few indications as to the location of certain fields named in this collection of charters. It seems likely that the fields recorded in 1725 as 'Home Common' and in 1769 as 'The Holme' and 'The Home' were in the fourteenth century the fields called 'Sutholm' and 'Northolm'. The root of Holme (ON *holmr*) meaning 'higher dry ground amid marshes', given the location, confirms this impression.[47] The area that on the map of 1725 is labelled 'Tuffs' (recorded as 'Tuffts' in the key to the map) and which lies outside the parish on the Honington side of the common, probably equates with the land known as 'le Toftyes' in the middle ages. And it is quite likely that the 'Bekfeld' of the fourteenth century was preserved in the field names of 'Beck', 'Upper Beck' and 'Lower Beck' of the eighteenth century. And it might be possible to suggest that the heath called 'Spinheth' in charters 58, 59, 82 and 159 lay to the west of the

43 SRO, Bury St Edmunds, P554.

44 Savery, 'Ixworth Thorpe', 51. There is a third area of medieval settlement south of Holms Wood around the field called 'Home Common' in 1725 and 'The Home' in 1769, though on balance this is probably not a significant site and certainly was not a centre of either medieval manor.

45 At the very end of our period there is evidence that there was some enclosure going on in the parish (171, 173).

46 SRO, Bury St Edmunds, P554 ('A survey made of the manor of Ixworth Thorpe for Thomas Crofts Reed esq. lord of the said manor the 22[d] Day of July 1725 geometrically described by Peter Fouloe') and M558 ('A map of the estate of Thomas Crofts Reade esq[r] lying in the parishes of Bardwell and Ixworth Thorpe &c: survey'd in the year of our LORD 1769 – by Parker of Thetford').

47 J. Field, *English Field-Names: a Dictionary*, Newton Abbot, Devon, 1972, 106.

Map 1. Ixworth Thorpe and its Surrounds

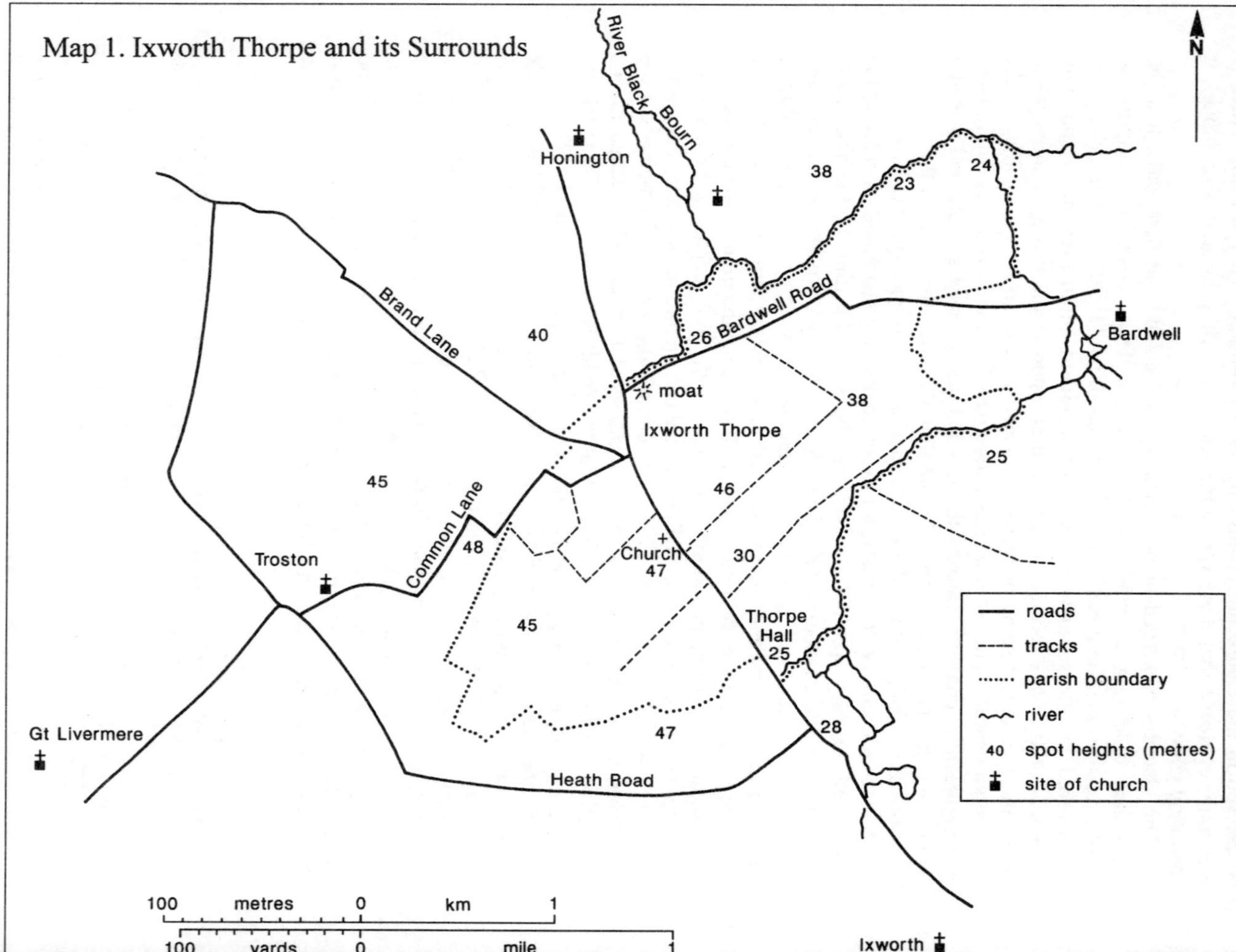

Map 2. The Parish of Ixworth Thorpe

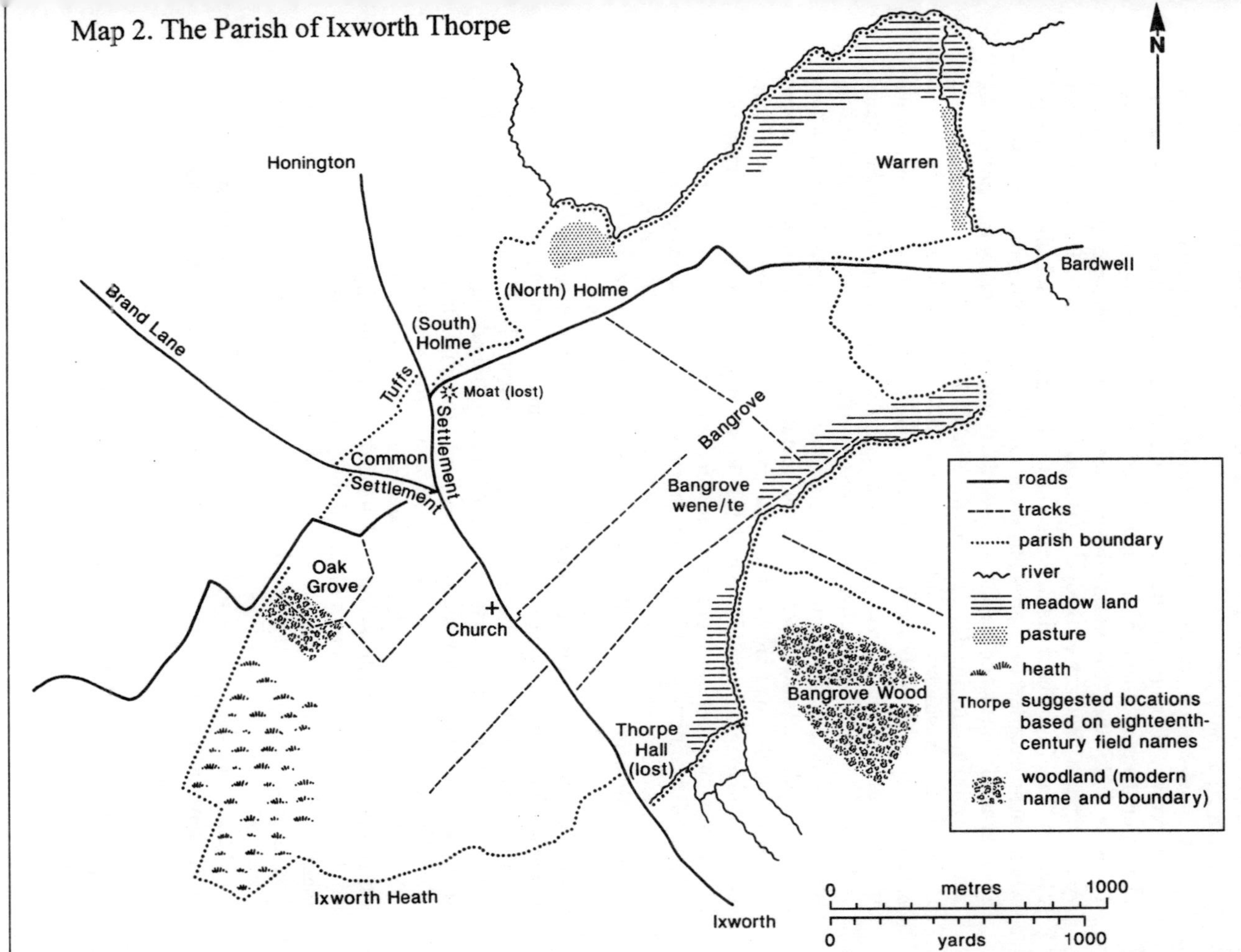

wood marked as 'Oak Grove' on Map 2. Firstly we know that this was the location of the heathland in the parish, secondly, the wood itself has evidence of a medieval origin,[48] and thirdly, the name (ME *spinney*) means 'heath containing or adjoining a copse'.[49]

The most certain identification, however, is in the placement of the fourteenth-century 'Brangravewene/te' and 'Bangrave'. These names were preserved almost unchanged down to the eighteenth century as 'Bangrow want' in three fields in 1725 and 'Great Bangrove Want', 'Little Bangrove Want', 'Twelve Acres against Bangrove Bridge', 'Bangrove Want', and 'Bangrove Bridge Meadow' in 1769. These fields were clustered around a track shown on Map 2 which must have led to a crossing point on the river between the parishes of Ixworth and Ixworth Thorpe and on towards, though presumably not through, the ancient woodland to this day called Bangrove Wood.[50]

There are a number of other features that are preserved in the eighteenth-century maps of Ixworth Thorpe and which must have been visible in the middle ages. The most obvious feature is the common around which the village of Ixworth Thorpe is now clustered. It must be this land (rather than the area in the south of the parish known as Easter Green)[51] that is referred to in the collection of charters printed here. Another feature that seems to have remained unchanged is the road layout. The main road that runs through the parish from Ixworth to Honington and known as the 'king's highway' in these charters (41, 91, 154) almost certainly preserves its medieval line, retaining, as it does, the reverse 'S' characteristic of a road abutting an open field system. Equally indicative of a medieval road is that which goes from Ixworth Thorpe to Bardwell. The series of 90° bends in the road probably reflect the original furlong boundaries of the open fields. And it is likely that the track that currently leads off in the direction of Bardwell from just south of Ixworth Thorpe church preserves, albeit in a straightened form, the line of the 'via' recorded in charter 118 from the church to Bardwell. The route from Ixworth Thorpe to Troston also has the characteristic series of 90° bends reflecting the original furlong boundaries making this, too, a likely site of a medieval track way. It is likely, too, that the wood now known as 'Oak Grove' ('Thorpe Grove' in 1769)[52] is ancient woodland. Its name (grove, OE *graf*), meaning a small managed woodland, its location on the high ground, on the edge of the parish and on land difficult to cultivate, and the fact that there are the probable remains of a medieval ditch and woodbank all point to the fact that this wood was in existence in the middle ages.[53] Ixworth Thorpe provides a fine testament to the way in which these features in the landscape can be preserved down the generations.

There is another feature that has been preserved in the eighteenth-century field-names and which would have been familiar to Sir William of Pakenham.

48 Field-walking has revealed the probable site of medieval ditch and woodbank.

49 Field, *Dictionary*, 214.

50 Also shown on two maps now in the possession of Mr John Cross of Dairy Farm, Ixworth, and dated 1625 and 1796. My thanks are due to Mr Cross for allowing me to see these maps.

51 See above p. 7.

52 SRO, Bury St Edmunds, M558.

53 O. Rackham, *Trees and Woodland in the British Landscape*, London 1990, 46, 112–16.

Knowledge of the warren was preserved in the eighteenth-century field-names of 'Middle Warren', 'Lower Warren', 'Pasture Warren' and 'Warren Car'.[54] This resource, located on the border of Bardwell parish, must have been of considerable size and would have provided ample testimony to the wealth and status of the owners of this manor. It may well have been here, too, that one of the mills that the estate enjoyed was located. It is certain that any water mills that existed must have been placed on the river and therefore the boundary of the estate, and it is here that on the 1769 map a mill is marked.

William of Pakenham's Career

Sir William first emerges into the light of the documentary evidence on 12 May 1259 when he obtained free-warren for his demesne lands in Ixworth Thorpe and Bardwell. This concession cost Sir William 5 marks and would in June 1292 be renewed and extended to cover his lands in Pakenham, Norton, and Fakenham Aspes.[55] Sir William was obviously a man on his way up.[56] In January 1260, however, Sir William's upward climb was unaccountably interrupted. On the 17th of that month, Roger de Turkelby was appointed to make an inquisition concerning Sir William's 'withdrawal from the realm'. The following July, Henry of Bath was ordered to carry out the inquiry to ascertain whether Sir William had left England 'through fear or because of some charge of felony, and if for felony, whether he was guilty thereof'.[57] Unfortunately the outcome of this inquiry is not known.

At some point between 1260 and 1270, Sir William can be found acting as a bailiff for the abbot of St Edmunds.[58] He also appears, somewhat surprisingly given his close connection to Bury, to have been at sometime a seneschal of the bishop of Norwich.[59] In the records of central government, however, Sir William only begins to appear on a regular basis in 1283. In July of that year with Roger Loveday he was sent on a commission of *oyer et terminer* (to hear and determine) concerning damage done to the parks of Roger Bigod during his absence on campaign in Wales.[60] After this assignment, Sir William was sent on a number of *oyer et terminer* cases in Suffolk and Norfolk,[61] including, in October 1290, one with William of Gislingham ordering them, 'without prejudice and at the instance of the abbot, and with the consent of the king's council', to inquire into

54 SRO, Bury St Edmunds, M558.

55 *Cal. Charter Rolls, 1257–1300*, 17, 422; a further grant of free warren was given to Thomas of Pakenham in June 1318 (*Cal. Charter Rolls, 1300–26*, 382). The significance of this grant is discussed above on pp. 5–6.

56 Bailey, 'The rabbit and the medieval East Anglian economy', 1–20.

57 *Cal. Patent Rolls, 1258–66*, 102 (*bis*).

58 M.D. Lobel, 'A list of the aldermen and bailiffs of Bury St Edmunds from the twelfth to the sixteenth century', *Proceedings of the Suffolk Institute of Archaeology*, 22 (1936), 17–28 (at 19).

59 *Rot. Hund.*, ii, 198.

60 *Cal. Patent Rolls, 1281–92*, 73.

61 *Cal. Patent Rolls, 1281–92*, 171, 184, 205 (*bis*), 279, 208, 344, 400, 406, 452; *The Letter-Book of William of Hoo, Sacrist of Bury St Edmunds 1280–1294*, ed. A. Gransden, Suffolk Records Society V, 1963, 34n, 35n, no. 21 and nn, 134, 135.

trespasses made by the men of Bury St Edmunds on the Saint's property.[62] As well as specific cases of *oyer et terminer*, Sir William may also be found on more general assizes. In August 1285, for example, he was ordered with William Burnton, Roger Loveday, and Nicholas de Gras to take assizes, juries, and inquisitions in Norfolk and Suffolk for three terms, viz: between 14 September and 6 October; between 6 January 1286 and 2 February; and between 8 July and 1 August.[63] Sir William also took part in commissions of gaol delivery in Norfolk and Suffolk.[64]

The commission of 18 October 1290 to look into the complaint made by the abbot of Bury St Edmunds seems to have been Sir William's last case, yet he was to live a further fourteen years. It may be that he had failed to please in his handling of the case or perhaps he fell foul of the so-called 'scandal of the judges' in 1290 in the wake of Edward I's return from Gascony.[65] In any event, it was not until 1299 that he can be found again operating outside his personal circles when on 2 February he was one of a number of named witnesses to the payment of 220 marks by the powerful men of Bury St Edmunds to the abbot as a means of bringing a dispute to an end.[66] Sir William also seems to have worked for St Edmunds. He can be found as one of the abbot's justices sitting at Bury,[67] and he witnessed at least two charters of Abbot John of Northwold, one dated certainly to 1289, the other probably of the same year.[68] We next hear of Sir William when a notice of his death was sent to the escheator on this side of the Trent in January 1305.[69]

The documents that were drawn up on Sir William's death give us an insight into the circumstances that must have surrounded his acquisition of his landed estates. We have already seen how in charter no. 4 the manor at Ixworth Thorpe seems to have descended to Sir William and his brother John by right of a grant made by their uncle, Mr John of Pakenham. And yet by 1280, neither John nor any putative heirs seem to have held an interest in the manor. On 28 April 1305 an enrolment was made in the king's chancery of a deed given by a certain William son of John of Pakenham on 22 April that year. [70] In this deed William son of John acknowledged that all the lands in Pakenham, Thurston, Barton, Livermere, Norton, Tostock, Stowlangtoft, Wattisfield, Ixworth Thorpe, and Beyton, Suffolk, and the manor of Belaugh, Norfolk, and the manor of Hunneshurst, Kent,[71] belonged to Sir William of Pakenham in return for a messuage, two carucates of land and 100 shillings yearly rent in the towns of Pakenham, Thurston, Norton, Bardwell and Stowlangtoft.[72] William son of John of Pakenham's son, also named John of Pakenham, ratified the agreement and

62 *Cal. Patent Rolls, 1281–92*, 389.
63 *Cal. Close Rolls, 1279–88*, 365.
64 *Cal. Patent Rolls, 1281–92*, 260, 264, 283, 284 (*bis*), 284–7; *Cal. Close Rolls, 1288–96*, 15.
65 Powicke, *Thirteenth Century*, 361–3.
66 *Pinchbeck*, i, 1–3.
67 M.D. Lobel, *The Borough of Bury St Edmunds*, Oxford 1937, 96.
68 CUL, Mm. iv. 19., fos 47v, 49v.
69 *Cal. Fine Rolls*, i, 507, 513.
70 *Cal. Close Rolls, 1302–7*, 329.
71 *CIPM*, vii, n. 436.
72 *Placitorum*, 259 b.

WILLIAM OF PAKENHAM AND HIS FAMILY

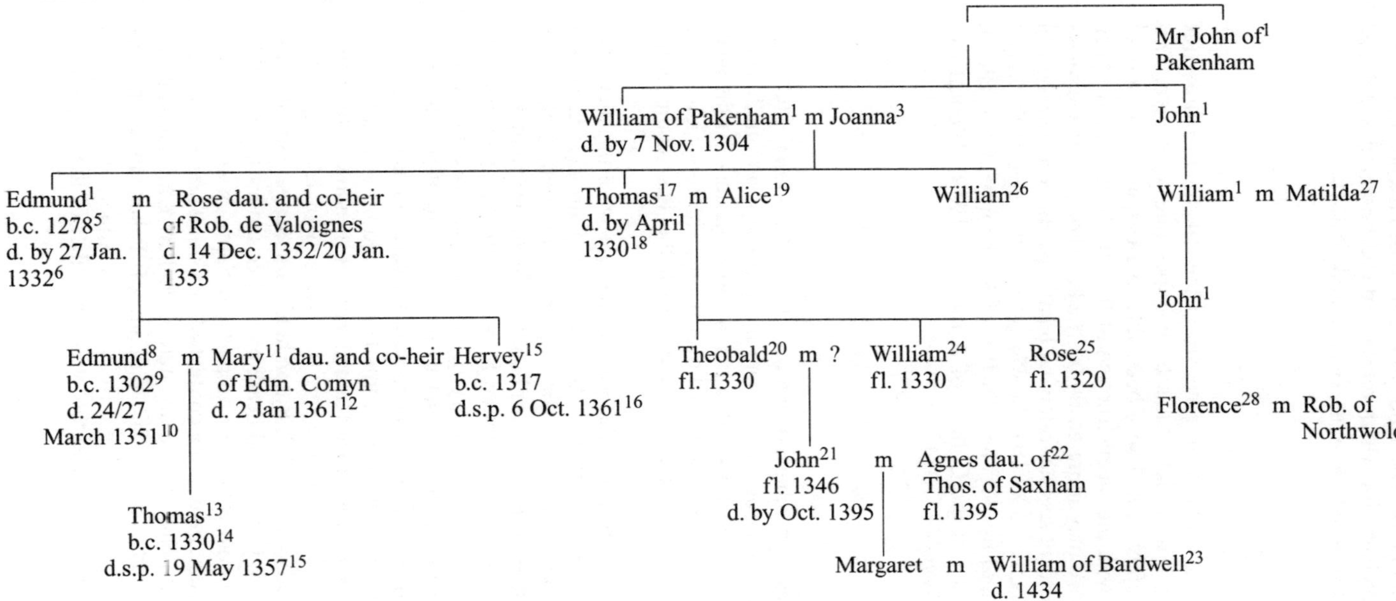

(N.B. Some notes refer to more than one entry)

1 No. 4; *Cal. Close Rolls, 1302–7*, 329.
2 Nos 6 and 131.
3 Nos 83, 86, 115, 116, 126.
4 *Cal. Close Rolls, 1307–13*, 301; *Cal. Patent Rolls, 1307–13*, 326; *Cal. Patent Rolls, 1317–21*, 74.
5 *CIPM*, iv, no. 293.
6 *Cal. Close Rolls, 1330–33*, 430.
7 *CIPM*, x, no. 111.
8 *Cal. Close Rolls, 1333–37*, 49.
9 *CIPM*, vii, no. 436.
10 *CIPM*, ix, no. 641.
11 *Cal. Close Rolls, 1349–54*, 412, 449.
12 *CIPM*, xi, no. 154.
13 *Cal. Fine Rolls, 1347–56*, 362, 370; *Cal. Patent Rolls, 1354–58*, 272.
14 *CIPM*, ix, no. 641.
15 *CIPM*, xi, no. 155; *Cal. Fine Rolls, 1356–69*, 171.
16 *CIPM*, xi, no. 156; *Cal. Close Rolls, 1307–13*, 301; *Cal. Patent Rolls, 1307–13*, 326.
17 Nos 6 and 131.
18 No. 169a.
19 Nos 1, 72 etc.
20 No. 165.
21 *Feudal Aids*, v, 72.
22 BL Harl. Charter, 54 F 7.
23 Copinger, *Manors*, 380–1.
24 Nos 165, 168, 169, 169a.
25 No. 167.
26 No. 5.
27 *Placitorum*, 259b.
28 *Cal. Close Rolls, 1302–7*, 325.

released all right that he had in the said lands to Edmund of Pakenham, son and heir of Sir William of Pakenham, for which release Edmund granted to John all the lands that he held in Drinkstone, Woolpit, Hessett and Tostock.

William of Pakenham and his Family

There have been a number of attempts to reconstruct the Pakenham family tree and all have problems, some of which it has been impossible to resolve. This particular family tree, therefore, is as I have been able to ascertain it. Because of the difficulties associated with the reconstruction of the family, notes have been attached so that the evidence may more easily be tracked. For alternative views on the Pakenham family descent see the following locations: BL Add. MS 19,144 (Davy's Suffolk Collections, vol. LXVIII); the west wall of the nave of St Mary's Church, Pakenham (compiled by W.L. and J.R.R.L. Pakenham with J.H. Bloom and registered by A.T. Butler at the College of Arms, Oct. 1939); Bloomfield, *Norfolk*, viii, 403; *Monasticon*, VI, i, 311–12.

Witnesses to the Charters

The core group of witnesses to the charters in this collection was relatively small. There were thirty-three or thirty-four men (there are problems surrounding the identification of William le Sire) who attested ten or more charters. At the heart of this group were thirteen men who witnessed over twenty charters each. These men represent the political and social circles in which the Pakenham family moved.

The most prolific attesters to this collection of charters were the men who witnessed in the presence of Sir William of Pakenham. First amongst these was Ralph of Bardwell who witnessed sixty-three charters in total. Ralph was undoubtedly a significant man in Blackbourn hundred. In the assize of 1285, he was one of the twenty-four jurymen appointed for the double hundred. In 1280, Ralph appeared as the son and heir of Henry of Bardwell and his then widow Margaret de Aula. In Hunston Ralph was set to inherit his mother's dower as capital lord of the vill, a messuage with more than 90 acres of land, meadow, pasture and wood (in 1283, the movables on this land would be valued at £9 2s 0d), and another portion of 36 acres of land and an acre of meadow in the hands of Margaret's villeins. In Bardwell itself, where the assessors of 1283 calculated his movables as being valued at £14 5s 3d, Ralph held a messuage with over 140 acres of arable land, meadow, pasture and heath plus other sundry lands held by his tenants. Ralph also had connections to property in Sapiston and Stanton.[73] Ralph was clearly an important man in the context of this small area of Suffolk.

Only pushed into second place by one attestation, Robert Ultra Aquam was the second most prolific attester of Sir William of Pakenham's charters (sixty-two in total). Like Ralph of Bardwell, Robert Ultra Aquam was a big fish in the Blackbourn hundred fishpond. He, too, was a member of the jury for the

73 *Suffolk Hundred*, tt. 3, 15; xix, 9, 29, 31–3, 44, 59, 76, 84, 85.

double hundred in 1285. His assessment in Bardwell in 1283 was £9 19s 6d and here he held a message with an acre of land, another parcel of 26 acres of arable land, pasture and meadow, and a further three parcels of land. He also had a connection with land held by the priory of Ixworth in Ixworth.[74]

William of Thelnetham witnessed fifty-one of the Pakenham charters (including a few of Thomas's). He, too, was one of the significant men of the hundred, being a juror in 1285 and having his movables in Troston assessed at £12 11s 0d in 1283. Here he held a message with over 40 acres of land, pasture and heath. And at Barnham in 1283, William had movables assessed at £3 14s 2d.[75] John son of William of Bardwell was also a significant man in the hundred. Although not a juror in 1285, he did hold large amounts of property in the area. At Bardwell in 1280 he held a message with 8 acres of arable land and in Stanton he held a message with an acre of land. His movables in Bardwell in 1283 were assessed at £21 13s 9d, placing him very much amongst the elite in the hundred.[76] In Sapiston, he had an assessment of £2 15s 0½d.[77]

Peter of Thorpe is the first of the major attesters (forty-six in total) who does not seem to have held significant amounts of land in the hundred. He held some land in Ixworth Thorpe, though how much is not made clear since his holding appears as an abuttal (68). Peter's major holding seems to have been at Pakenham itself, in the neighbouring hundred of Thedwestre, where he held 30 acres of the abbot of St Edmunds.[78] This was, of course, a major centre of William of Pakenham's lands, and Peter's presence in so many charter witness-lists relating to land in Ixworth Thorpe must reflect the fact that the Pakenhams held him in high esteem.

These five men were the most constant witnesses to Sir William of Pakenham's charters, but there was a second tier of men who were also close to him. Simon of Gislingham witnessed twenty-seven charters and also sold a number of pieces of land to Sir William in Ixworth Thorpe and Honington (25–36). He held land in Ixworth Thorpe, Honington, Troston and Stanton,[79] and in 1283 his movables in Ixworth Thorpe were assessed at £2 1s 10d.[80] Also important in this second group of attesters was Ralph son of Simon of Thorpe. Unfortunately nothing other than what is available in the charters is known about Ralph. From this source we know that he held land in Ixworth Thorpe, though how much is not clear (85 and 97 are abuttals and 91 concerns a rent). Likewise Adam de Suthenton was an important witness to Sir William's charters (twenty-six in total). In 1280, he held a message in Barningham and a small parcel of

74 *Suffolk Hundred*, t. 4; xix, 13, 31, 32.

75 *Suffolk Hundred*, tt. 5, 32; xix, 38.

76 *Suffolk Hundred*, xx. The assessment table reads as follows: William of Pakenham £108 12s 6d; William Criketot £49 19s 0d; Peter of Thelnetham £40; a further 5 owners assessed at between £20 and £30; and 28 owners at between £10 and £20. John son of William of Bardwell was in the top eight, therefore.

77 *Suffolk Hundred*, tt. 4, 26; 31, 51.

78 *Pinchbeck*, ii, 142.

79 Rye, *FF Suffolk*, 77, 107.

80 *Suffolk Hundred*, t. 31.

land in Stowlangtoft. On the land in Stowlangtoft his widow had movables assessed at £1 13s 2d in 1283.[81] And Robert le Sire witnessed twenty-two of Sir William's charters. The Sire family were important land owners in Ixworth Thorpe, holding movables assessed at £3 2s 0d and £1 19s 4d in 1283, and William le Sire was an important tenant of St Edmunds in the vill.[82]

By the time of Sir William's death, age and perhaps also Thomas's personal preference was beginning to take its toll on the men who had stayed with William throughout most of his life. By 1300, Ralph of Bardwell was dead, to be succeeded in his lands by his son Henry.[83] Robert Ultra Aquam witnessed no charters that are demonstrably later than 1300, before which time he must have died, presumably shortly after December 1293, the latest date given on any of the charters he witnessed (24). William of Thelnetham managed to outlast Sir William. As we might expect, therefore, he was at Norton to witness Sir William's son William quitclaim to his father all right that he had in Ixworth Thorpe (5) and he was also there to witness the act by which Sir William's eldest son, Edmund, granted to Thomas the land that was to make up his inheritance (6). He is not to be found, though, as a witness to Thomas of Pakenham's charters, suggesting perhaps that he was out of favour with Sir William's younger son. Also present on the two occasions that the succession to Ixworth Thorpe was determined was Peter of Thorpe. He, however, can be found witnessing two of Thomas's charters, the second dated in January 1307 (23, 79).

John son of William of Bardwell was not present at the meetings in 1304; he did, though, witness three of Thomas's charters, the last dating from July 1310 (23, 101, 155). Of the other members of the group that accompanied Sir William through his life, Simon of Gislingham was dead by 1303/4,[84] Ralph son of Simon witnessed nothing that dates after December 1293 (24), and in fact was part of an even older generation that was around to witness charters before 1263 (43, 62, 105). He, presumably, was dead by the autumn of 1304. Likewise, Robert le Sire witnessed nothing after December 1293 (24); he, too, was part of the pre-1263 generation (18). Richard de Suthenton had died in the winter months of 1282–3.[85]

There was now a new generation to surround the man of the moment, Thomas of Pakenham, and these new men were led by Walter Kenne. Although Walter was around to witness a few of the pre-Thomas charters (22, 24, 71, 75, 142), he was not one of Sir William's regular attesters despite holding land in Ixworth Thorpe by 1282 (32, where his land appears as an abuttal) and granting land in the vill to Sir William before and after 1290 (55, 56). In 1283 his movables here were assessed at £3 12s 3d. He also shared with Thomas de la Dale four sheep assessed at 2s 6d.[86] The vast majority of his attestations (thirty-five in total) date

81 *Suffolk Hundred*, 19, 31; t. 29.

82 *Suffolk Hundred*, t. 31; 44.

83 *Pinchbeck*, i, 276.

84 Rye, *FF Suffolk*, 107.

85 See below in 'Biographical List'.

86 *Suffolk Hundred*, t. 31 (*bis*). In Stanton he was styled 'capellanus' where he held movables assessed at £2 10s 0d. In 1280, it was said he held there 1½ acres of land for a rent of ¼d (ibid. t. 27; 50).

to the years of Thomas's hold over Ixworth Thorpe. The latest dated charter to which he appended his name was 25 January 1312 (154), though he was mentioned in a grant that must date to no earlier than 1315 (166).

Less obviously part of this new generation, but still a man who was peripheral to Sir William's circle of friends, Robert son of Ralph of Ixworth Thorpe also witnessed thirty-five charters. Ten of these charters date from before Sir William's death (20, 22, 45, 56, 71, 73, 86, 128, 129, 142), the remaining twenty-five date from 1305 to 6 October 1314 (1), though he was involved in a sale that must be dated after this deed (166). He, like Walter Kenne, held land in Ixworth Thorpe (81, 120, 136, 137, 145, 146, 153, 159, 160, 164–6). Robert de le Hil of Bardwell was also important in the circle of Thomas's friends. He witnessed sixteen charters, all in the post-1304 period. Robert's first attestation occurred on 1 May 1307 (136) and his last on 24 June 1315 (171). And given his name and place of abode, it is likely that he is a descendant of the Thomas de la Hill who in 1283 had movables assessed at £2 16s 6d in Bardwell.[87]

There were men, of course, who did manage to span the divide of 1304, though apart from Sir Peter of Thelnetham (twenty-one in total) and William le Warde (twenty in total), none of these men were in the twenty-plus attestation league.[88] Sir Peter's twenty-one attestations were divided seven before Sir William's death and fourteen after. Sir Peter was also at the two meetings at which the descent of Ixworth Thorpe was determined (5, 6). He was, however, one of the three major secular potentates in Blackbourn hundred (his movables in 1283 being assessed at £40 in Thelnetham). In 1280, Sir Peter is recorded as having extensive interests in the hundred.[89] Presumably, therefore, Sir Peter's presence as a witness to many of the transactions throughout this period was a reflection of the importance of his participation in the proceedings. William le Warde also crossed the divide and perhaps this, too, indicates his significance to the Pakenhams. His attestations are divided almost equally between the two periods, eleven before Sir William's death and nine after. It maybe that he was a descendant of Ralph le Warde who held movables in Market Weston in 1283 assessed at £3 15s 8d and who in 1285 was a juror of the double hundred of Blackbourn and Bradmere.[90] What is certain is that he was a major seller of property to the Pakenhams. His is the very first charter recorded in the cartulary (1) and its presence in this position is difficult to explain other than in terms of a simple mistake or, though perhaps less likely, in terms of an indicator as to its importance to compiler of the cartulary.[91] Leaving this rather dubious suggestion aside, it is plain that William le Warde's sales to the Pakenhams were important. From the evidence in the cartulary, we know that William was selling land to Sir William before 1290 (17, 19, 20, 21), sales that cost Sir William £9. He also sold eight further pieces of land to Thomas for unspecified amounts (1, 72, 120, 137, 151, 157, 162, 167). And in his final sale to Thomas, he played a part in the

87 *Suffolk Hundred*, t. 4.

88 For a summary of the attestations of these men including all those who witnessed ten or more charters see Biographical List, below.

89 *Suffolk Hundred*, t. 30, xx, 27, 31, 36–39, 41, 45.

90 *Suffolk Hundred*, xix, t. 22.

91 For a discussion of the organisation of the material in the cartulary see below, pp. 18–20.

establishment of property for Thomas and Alice's daughter Rose, and even at this point he had not exhausted his assets in Ixworth Thorpe (167). William le Warde was obviously a neighbour whom the Pakenhams could not ignore.

What emerges from this brief survey of the men who witnessed the Pakenham purchases in Ixworth Thorpe is that they were local men to their core. Indeed, most of these men held land actually in Ixworth Thorpe and its very immediate surrounds. This was the society in which Sir William of Pakenham and his son Thomas moved.

The Cartulary

British Library Campbell Charters XVII comprises thirty-four folios of vellum each measuring 283mm x 222mm.[92] The first 31 folios encompass the 178 deeds calendared in this edition. Fos 32, 33 and 34 contain separate pieces of account rolls: fos 32 and 33 are very fragmentary; fo. 34, while being better preserved, gives little indication as to its purpose or provenance. But since the current binding is later than the compilation of the cartulary (probably post medieval) and the cartulary seems to have found its way into the hands of Ixworth priory along with the manor in the fifteenth century, the accounts may well have nothing to do with the Pakenham family. There seem to have been at least two scribes: the main scribe, who wrote up the documents to fo. 28r and from fo. 29v to 31r, and the second scribe, who wrote the documents from 28v to 29r.[93]

The cartulary was wrongly bound at some point before the early notation. Modern fo. 21r should follow fo. 16v as is shown by the continuation of charter 90 at the top of fo. 21r. Fos 22, 23 and 24 were also misbound, presumably at the same time, and should follow fo. 21. The evidence for this misbinding is twofold. The first is that, as is explained in more detail below, the compiler of the cartulary worked to a number of themes in organising his documents, the most important of which was by major recipient. The documents on fos 22–24 relate to acquisitions by Sir William of Pakenham and yet the current organisation places them in the group of Thomas of Pakenham's purchases. The second is that documents 141, 142, 143 and 144 belong together as a group, referring as they do to the same piece of meadow. Yet the current binding would have nos 141, 142 and 143 on fo. 20v and no. 144 on fo. 25r. The arrangement of the cartulary as represented by the current binding cannot, therefore, be allowed to stand, and the cartulary has been rearranged in this edition to conform to the original plan of the compiler.[94]

The cartulary is organised on a number of levels: the first and most obvious way is by the two major recipients of grants, Sir William of Pakenham and Thomas of Pakenham. With a few exceptions the documents in the cartulary up to no. 131 relate to Sir William's transactions in the land market and those from

92 No. 1304 in G.R.C. Davis, *Medieval Cartularies of Great Britain: a Short Catalogue*, London 1958, 151.

93 The main scribe has a characteristic lower-case 'g', with its descender turning outward like a modern 'q', while the second scribe employs the more usual fourteenth-century 'g'.

94 See p. xiv.

132, again with a few exceptions, relate to the activities of Thomas. Within the bounds of this theme, the compiler wished to stress the importance of the series of grants that lay the foundations for the Pakenham holding at Ixworth Thorpe by placing them early in the cartulary. For this reason he has transcribed as nos 4, 5 and 6 the grants that made up the basis of Thomas's holding in Ixworth Thorpe.

The third major theme in the organisation of the cartulary is by grantor. The scribe's method seems to have been to bring together all the documents relating to an individual or group of related individuals and to write them up in a block. And, where he had access to them, the compiler would also include in the block any related documents, such as an earlier grant to the grantor or a quitclaim by a relative concerning the land granted. So, for example, the documents relating to the lands granted by Simon of Gislingham to Sir William of Pakenham appear as nos 25–36. Nos 32, 33, 34 and 35 stand alone without any accompanying documents. No. 25, however, is a grant in heredity by Simon of Gislingham to Richard son of Matilda le Ros of 5 acres of land in Honington, no. 29 is the quitclaim by which Richard gave up his right in the land he had bought from Simon, and no. 28 is the grant in heredity selling the land to Sir William. Again this pattern can be seen in nos 27, 30 and 36. No. 30 is a grant in heredity by William son of Nicholas le Ros to Simon of Gislingham of an acre of arable land in the field called Longfurlong to hold of the grantor for 2d p.a., no. 27 is the grant in heredity by which Simon handed over this land to Sir William to be held of Simon for 2d p.a., and no. 36 is the quitclaim by which Simon gave up his right in the 2d of annual rent. This theme is continued with the grants made by Geoffrey of Thorpe and his family to Sir William with nos 37–52 relating to the land bought from Geoffrey and his family.

Later on, too, this theme is again picked up in the grants to Thomas of Pakenham and his wife. For example, nos 141, 142, 143 and 144 all relate to the same piece of meadow: no. 142 is a quitclaim by which a certain Richard Armerard gave up all his right in the meadow to Robert Knight; no. 143 is the grant in heredity by Alice widow of Robert Knight to Thomas of Pakenham and his wife Alice; no. 141 is the quitclaim by which William son of Robert Knight gave up his rights in the meadow; and no. 144 is the quitclaim by which Adam Armerard, Alice Knight's brother and presumably Richard Armerard's heir, though not his son as the document makes clear, gave up his claim to the meadow.

This arrangement has some benefits for us; for example, it allows us to 'imagine' that Alice daughter of Geoffrey of Thorpe may well have been the same person as Alice widow of Ralph Cassamerre. Her charters to Sir William are arranged as nos 7, 8, 10, 11, 13, 14 and 15. No. 9 is a grant in heredity by William son of Ralph Cassamerre of 1½ acres of arable land in Ixworth Thorpe and no. 12 is a quitclaim by Alice widow of Ralph Cassamerre to William son of Ralph of Cassemerre of all right in the aforementioned 1½ acres.

Nonetheless, despite this seemingly clear organisation, the arrangement of the cartulary does present some difficulties. For example, the four charters that determine the inheritance of the Blund land and the descent of the whole manor to Thomas and which we might have expected to come first – the grant of Mr John of Pakenham to his nephews of Ixworth Thorpe (4); the quitclaim by William son of Sir William of Pakenham of his interests in the manor (5); the grant in heredity by Edmund of Pakenham to Thomas and his heirs of the manor

(6); and the mandate by Edmund to the free tenants and others of the manor to submit to Thomas (131) – do not. In the case of no. 131, the compiler seems to have been working to a more important theme. Here he used this mandate to indicate that he was beginning the second part of his first major organisational theme, viz. by major recipient. But why should nos 4, 5 and 6 appear as such and not as nos 1, 2 and 3? Alas I do not have an answer. Equally, I have not been able to fathom why no. 1 (a grant in heredity by William le Warde to Thomas and Alice of a parcel of land in *Wardishamus toft* field) or no. 2 (a quitclaim by John of Aveney to Richard of Barnham of all right in 4s of annual rent) or no. 3 (another quitclaim by John to Richard of all suit of court for a meadow) should have pride of place as the first items in the cartulary. They do not seem to fit the compiler's first, second, or third major themes. Moreover, they seem to concern relatively small grants when compared to the major grants that we meet in this cartulary. These documents do, however, comprise the whole of the first side of fo. 1 while no. 4 starts the verso of that folio. At the bottom of fo. 1r there is a gap of more than 60mm. Under normal circumstances our main scribe (whose script this is) would have started the next document on this folio rather than wasting valuable vellum. It is perhaps worth noting that fo. 1r has the appearance have having had an extended period of exposure without the benefit of being covered by a binding.

The overall arrangement of this cartulary does tell us something meaningful about the priorities of our compiler and his patron, Thomas of Pakenham. It seems that their aim was to demonstrate how the land at Ixworth Thorpe had been acquired.[95] Perhaps because the documents contained in the Pakenham cartulary relate to just one manor it was felt unnecessary or even undesirable to arrange the material topographically. Whatever the case, grants relating to the same piece of land can be masked by the overriding concerns of the compiler. For example, in August 1310 Thomas of Pakenham exchanged land at Honington with Walter Kenne and William his son for land at Ixworth Thorpe (158). The land at Honington comprised mostly lands that Sir William of Pakenham had acquired from Simon of Gislingham thirty years before (28, cf. 25, 29), but the arrangement of the cartulary makes this fact difficult to see without considerable effort.

At the end of the manuscript there are two sets of notation that do little other than tantalise the editor. The first, at the base of membrane 31r, is the date 1321 in Arabic numerals in a script characteristic of the sixteenth century, though this is obviously a tentative observation since there is so little material with which to judge the date. 1321 is most certainly a date that would fit within the bounds of when the cartulary could have been drawn up,[96] but on what evidence the date was assigned is, alas, no longer clear.

The second notation occurs on the dorse of membrane 31 and its transcription

95 Unlike most monastic cartularies (D. Walker, 'The organization of material in medieval cartularies', in *The Study of Medieval Records: Essays in Honour of Kathleen Major*, ed. D.A. Bullough and R.L. Story, Oxford 1971, 132–50) or, indeed, lay cartularies (see, for example, *The Langley Cartulary*, ed. P.R. Coss, Dugdale Society, vol. 32 (1980), xi).

96 See the following section, 'Date of the Cartulary'.

and reading are very problematical.[97] In a line from left to right, starting at the far left hand side of the membrane, someone has written a series of what appear to be Roman numerals separated by full stops. It seems to read 'x.x.x xxiii.xix.xx'. This is then followed by a series of letters that could conceivably read 'R. R(with a tail) E. Q. ff R. Haix'; or perhaps 'R. R(with a tail) E. N ff R. Haip(ro)'. This is then followed by the phrase 'usque adxxxiii fuit dominus Willelmus de Pakenham'. The third element of the phrase has the most obvious meaning: 'up to no. 33 it was William of Pakenham'. The reconstructed order of the cartulary allows one to say that the writer was referring to charters 1–133, which indeed, broadly speaking, refer to William of Pakenham's lands. In this instance we could allow a sloppy Latinist who had looked only cursorily at the manuscript in its pre-misbound days to be indicating that documents to 133 referred to belongings once held by William of Pakenham. The first two elements of the phrase remain even more enigmatic. Is the second part a dating clause of some description (though none that I have seen before)? And who might be Q (or conceivably N) son or daughter of R of Haix? After a trawl through the British Library's Index Nominum revealed no Haix or, indeed, an appropriate Hays or its variant, we were left none the wiser. And what do the Roman numerals signify?

Date of the Cartulary

The date of the very first charter copied up gives us a *terminus ad quem* for the compilation of 6 October 1314. None of the charters in the main scribe's hand up to fo. 28r date from after this point in time. Of the documents in the second scribe's hand, fos 28v to 29r, the latest dated charter is 6 November 1313 (165), though three of these documents might conceivably be dated after this point (166, 167, 168). No. 165 is the latest dated document (apart, obviously, from no. 1) up to this point in the manuscript. When the main scribe took up his task again on fo. 29v it was to record the last documents of the cartulary and these in the main postdate the November 1313 document (165). These documents are dated 7 November 1315 (169); 24 June 1315 (171); 10 June 1319 (173); 7 Feb 1317 (174); 10 June 1319 (175); 3 November 1318 (176); 1 November 1318 (177). Nos 170 and 172 do not have dating clauses in this manuscript. And no. 178, the last document to be recorded in the cartulary and dateable to before 1290, was presumably a miscellaneous charter that surfaced during this phase of compilation.

In the light of this evidence we might surmise that there were probably two distinct phases of compilation. The first phase, undertaken in the winter months of 1314–15, certainly included all the documents up to fo. 28r and probably, too, those documents up to fo. 29r. Although there is a change of hand between fo. 28r and 28v, document 163 runs over the two sides of the folio suggesting that the second scribe took up his task immediately after the main scribe had put down

97 Dr Michelle Brown and I spent a happy hour one Saturday trying to fathom this one. That we got anywhere near to understanding its significance is in large part due to her knowledge and experience.

his pen. The second phase of writing, again undertaken by the main scribe, seemingly occurred sometime after the date of the two charters dated 10 June 1319 (173, 175). This phase would certainly have been over by 1330 by which time Thomas of Pakenham, for whom the cartulary was created, was dead (169a). The charter of 1330 that reveals the fact of his death and in which John le Sire granted to Alice, Thomas's widow, and William their son a piece of land in Ixworth Thorpe which was to descend to William and then to Thomas's rightful heirs, is precisely the sort of document that should have found its way into this cartulary had the volume been drawn up after 1330. The date of 1321 given by the Arabic numerals preserved at the end of fo. 31r could, therefore, be right for the second phase of compilation. It is certainly within the bounds of possibility.

Accuracy and Completeness

There survive seven original charters from which the accuracy of the cartulary can be checked (6, 18, 19, 79, 112, 158, 171). The original of no. 19 is too fragmentary to be of any use, but the other originals show that the standard of our main scribe's copying was very high indeed. There are occasional slips in copying, inevitably, such as when in the witness list to no. 6 he omitted Richard of Felmingham's title of *magister* and when in no. 119 he elided two clauses to make a nonsense of this part of the charter, but errors of this nature are few and far between.

The question of whether our main scribe habitually curtailed his witness lists is a more difficult one to answer. In his contribution to the first phase of compilation (to half way through no. 163), he clearly did not shorten the witness lists of nos 6, 18, 19, 79 and 158. No. 112, however, has been clipped of over half its witnesses. We may surmise from this evidence that in the majority of instances, our main scribe was careful to record all the witnesses to his documents. When the main scribe returned to his task some years later (169), he became much more willing to cut out the apparently superfluous. In no. 171, for example, a charter for which we have the original, he has left out the witness list and the dating clause, preferring instead the phrase 'in cuius etcetera'. He used a similar phrase to exclude witness lists and/or dating clauses in nos 170, 174, 177 and 178. In no. 172 he used the phrase 'data etcetera, anno etcetera', and in no. 176 he simply put 'testibus'. The second scribe was more willing to cut witness lists and omit dating clauses. He was responsible for half of no. 163 and nos 164 to 168. Nos 167 and 168 have neither witnesses recorded nor a dating clause, no. 166 has no dating clause, though this could conceivably represent a lack in the original from which he made his copy. The second scribe was also quite willing to abbreviate his documents when he thought it appropriate. No. 167, for example, in which Thomas and Alice made some provision for their daughter Rose, is very heavily shortened; the meaning of the charter, however, has been preserved. Evidently, both scribes knew their business.

Editorial Method

The charters contained in this volume date from after 1250 so, in accordance with the original plan for *Suffolk Charters*, they are calendared in English. The diplomatic formulae, however, have been retained where possible on the basis that it is not the 'editor's function to save the reader the trouble of interpreting the documents', but to provide him or her with the material from which to form his or her own judgements.[98] Witness lists are retained in the form in which they appear in the manuscript. In the main body of the text, identifiable place-names have been modernised with the original form being placed in brackets. The exception to this rule has been Ixworth Thorpe itself where variant readings have been pulled together in the index, unless it appears as a toponymic. Likewise, *Pakynham* has been rendered as Pakenham without any further comment. Headings, footnotes and marginal notes are mentioned only when they add information not contained in the text. Post-medieval endorsements are not noted. All documents are in Latin unless otherwise stated. As in earlier volumes of *Suffolk Charters*, 'quondam' has been translated as 'formerly of', though it might equally have been translated as 'of the late'. In an attempt to maintain consistency, 'via' has been translated as 'road' even when, from the context, it is likely that the word refers to the ways along the furlongs of the strip-field system. The reader has been left to determine just what sort of 'via' is being described in the documents. In the transcription of place-names, and in particular the names of local fields and landmarks now mostly lost, I have had to deal with the perennial problem of distinguishing between the medieval forms of 'u', 'n', 'v', 'm', 'ui', 'in' etc. Without a place-name volume for Suffolk, the task has been made especially difficult and I have had to resort to my paleographical skills for a reading; I would caution the reader that I must often have got the form wrong. Surviving loose charters, including feet of fines, that were not included in the cartulary but which seem to be relevant to this cartulary have been inserted at the appropriate points and given 'A' numbers.

There are a number of Latin terms that appear repeatedly throughout the text and which have been translated as follows: *clavum gariophilii*, clove; *gersuma*, entry fine; *magister*, Master; *pre manibus*, in cash; *tenendum et habendum*, to hold and to have.

A Note on Surnames

The documents preserved in this cartulary date from a period in which there was still some fluidity in the practice of using surnames. Among the knightly class, the majority of families had surnames that were to follow them down the generations. Below that class, among the freeholders of East Anglian society, surnames

98 The clearest exposition of the principles of calendaring medieval documents is still to be found in the *Calendar of Antrobus Deeds before 1625*, ed. R.B. Pugh, Wiltshire Record Society, vol. 3, 1947.

were also gradually becoming hereditary in the thirteenth century. The men and women who appear in this cartulary, therefore, have been indexed under their surnames.

There is, however, one class of surnames that can cause particular difficulty. Occupational surnames were becoming more common by the end of the thirteenth century and by the early fourteenth century 'many were probably hereditary'. But we cannot always be certain that an occupational surname had become hereditary at this date. In an attempt to be consistent, however, I have assumed that occupational surnames had become hereditary with two exceptions. The first exception is that of *capellanus*, which in this cartulary seems to have been universally related to a man's current occupation. The second exception is in cases where the occupational appellation certainly refers to a person's job. In order to aid searches through the index, occupational surnames, for example *Sutor*, have been cross referenced to named individuals, for example Alexander the cobbler. In rendering names in the text, I have used 'of' when the toponymic is identifiable as a modern place-name, as in William of Pakenham, and 'de' where it is not identifiable, as in Richard de Suthenton. In the use of *dominus*, I have rendered it in its Latin form leaving it to the reader to decide if it should be translated as 'lord' or 'sir'. *Dominus* has been inserted only on the first occasion that it appears in any particular charter, unless its presence aids the reading of the text.

On the issue of how to render in the index the various ways in which the scribes referred to Ixworth Thorpe, I have decided to as far as possible follow the practice of contemporaries. Where Ixworth Thorpe is a place-name, it has been indexed under Ixworth Thorpe; where it is a surname, it has been indexed under Thorpe. This practice allows the solution of two problems: firstly, it allows me to index men and women by their known surname of Thorpe rather than 'modernising' it in such a way as to be positively misleading about contemporary practice; and secondly, it allows me to avoid having to index a man like Peter of Thorpe under Ixworth Thorpe when it is not at all clear that he came from that vill.

Criteria for Dating

As has been indicated earlier in this introduction, the charters that constitute this cartulary are very tightly focused both in time and place. The result of this is that a large number of individuals regularly appear as witnesses to the charters. Richard de Suthentun, for example, died sometime in the winter of 1283 (an event that, irritating though it must have been for him, provides valuable dating evidence for us), and witnessed no fewer than twenty-five of the cartulary charters; for twenty-three of these charters his attestation is central to the assigning of a date. But to repeat biographical information at the foot of each and every charter concerning Richard and others whose attestations help in dating them would be repetitive and wasteful of valuable space. The small amount that is known about each of the attestees and of the men and women who appear in the texts of these charters has, therefore, been summarised in the section headed 'Biographical List'. Each charter has a date or range of dates assigned to it. Where that date appears as a dating clause, it has been taken directly from the charter it concerns. Where that date appears in square brackets, it has been assigned it on the basis of the biographical material presented in this section. In addition, where evidence from the lives of the main protagonists in this cartulary, the Pakenhams, bears on the dating of a charter, this has been used.

There is also diplomatic evidence that has been used in the dating of some of the documents in this collection. The statute *Quia Emptores,* issued by Edward I in 1290, has long been seen as one of the 'great statutes' of Edward I's reign.[99] The aim of the promulgation was to bring to an end the practice of creating sub-tenancies. It was the creation of these sub-tenancies that had caused discomfort to the lordly elite in English society as they lost access to 'their escheats, marriages and wardships as a result of the machinations of their tenants'. *Quia Emptores* was designed to put right this situation and to force buyers of land in the thriving land market of late thirteenth-century England to hold their purchases directly of the lord of the land concerned. There was to be no escaping the obligations that the holding of land brought in Edward I's England.[100]

But what effect did *Quia Emptores* have on the diplomatic form of grants in heredity given in fee simple? In a formulary book written around the year 1300, the author reminded his audience that in a recent prohibition it had been decreed that it was no longer possible to put anyone between the capital lord of the fee and the tenant. Henceforward it was not acceptable to write 'habendum et tenendum de me et heredibus meis' nor 'reddendo mihi et heredibus meis'; on the contrary the scribe must write '[habendum et tenendum de] capitalibus dominis feodi servicia etc'.[101] A 'reminder' in a formulary book ten years after the statute might lead one to imagine that the law was being flouted, but this was not so in Ixworth Thorpe. In the documents included in this cartulary, we have evidence that the change in diplomatic form happened almost at once. The first datable charter after 30 November 1290 (the date from which the statute was to take effect), no. 116, dated 23 September 1291, has the new clause, as do all subsequent grants in heredity in fee simple.[102] There are no datable examples in this cartulary of the phrase *tenendum et habendum de capitalibus* etc. from before 1290, though it should be noted that some lords before 1290 could and sometimes did demand that their lands be held of the capital lords.[103]

99 As for all things medieval and legal, the starting point is F. Pollock and F.W. Maitland, *The History of English Law before the Time of Edward I*, 2 vols., Cambridge, 2nd edn, 1898, i, 337, 355; ii, 293. The assessment is from T.F.T. Plucknett, *Legislation of Edward I: the Ford Lectures for 1947*, Oxford 1949 on *Quia Emptores*, 102–8. For a page-and-a-half summary in plain English see R.E. Megarry and H.W.R. Wade, *The Law of Real Property*, London, 3rd edn, 1966, 32–3 (modern editions do not include the useful historical introductions).

100 The text is in *Statutes of the Realm*, 11 vols., ed. A. Luders *et al.*, Record Commission, London, 1810, i, 106. There is a convenient translation in *English Historical Documents, iii, 1189–1327*, ed. H. Rothwell, London 1975, no. 64. The text states that the change was to take effect from 30 Nov. 1290.

101 *Legal and Manorial Formularies Edited in Memory of J. Gilson*, Oxford 1933 [ed. A.J. Collins, B. Schofield and S.C. Ratcliff], 1. For a fuller explanation of how this change had an impact on landholding see A.W.B. Simpson, *A History of the Land Law*, Oxford, 2nd edn, 1986, 22, 54–5, 58, 77–9.

102 Grants in fee tail could, according to the statute, still be subinfeudated. This was the way in which Edmund of Pakenham bestowed Ixworth Thorpe on Thomas his brother in 1304 (6).

103 In dating the charters of the villeins of Peterborough abbey, the editors noticed that the statute *Quia Emptores* had an effect on the drafting of the conveyancing acts even of this class. They

Introduction

The reconstruction by codicological techniques of the process by which the cartulary was compiled has allowed a more accurate range of dates to be assigned to five charters that appear at the end of this document (166, 167, 168, 170, 172). These five charters must have been drawn up after the first phase of writing ended in the winter months of 1314–15,[104] and so have been assigned a range of dates to fit in with that analysis.

It should be pointed out that the List does not contain the biographical details of all men and women who appear in this collection of charters. It does not, moreover, contain every known detail of their lives and so should not be used as a last place of reference for these individuals. This section is designed simply to aid the process of dating the charters contained in this cartulary.

Biographical List

The list is organised alphabetically by toponymic or patronymic.

William son of ADAM held movables to the value of £5 5s 6d in Hinderclay and £2 7s 6d in Ixworth Thorpe (*Suffolk Hundred*, tt. 12, 31). He witnessed nos 7, 9 (16 March 1281), 11 (11 Jan. 1283), 13, 15, 33 (10 Nov. 1282), 35, 99, 106 and appeared in the texts of 11, 16 (as grantor), 94, 99.

Peter of AMPTON appeared in 1234/5 (Rye, *FF Suffolk*, 33).

Margaret de AULA appeared in the return of 1280 as the chief lord (*domina*) of Hunston; she held movables assessed at £9 2s 0d in the same vill in 1283, and in 1285/6 described herself as the widow of Henry of Bardwell (*Suffolk Hundred*, 9; t. 15; 84–5). She appeared in the texts of 101 (8 July 1305, by which time she was dead), 104.

John BALDWIN held movables assessed at 11s 4d in Ixworth in 1283 (*Suffolk Hundred*, t. 18). He appeared in the texts of 69 (as grantor), 106 (as grantor).

Ralph of BARDWELL was described as the son of Margaret de Aula and the late Henry of Bardwell in 1285/6 (*Suffolk Hundred*, 84–5). Ralph was dead by 1300 when his son Henry was holding in Bardwell, Hunston, Histon and Barningham (*Pinchbeck*, i, 276). He witnessed nos 7–8, 9 (16 March 1281), 10 (10 Nov. 1282), 11 (11 Jan. 1283), 13, 15, 17, 19–21, 24 (15 Dec. 1293), 25, 27, 28, 30–1, 33 (10 Nov. 1282), 34–5, 41 (28 April 1271), 42, 45, 54 (30 Aug. 1294), 55–61, 65, 68–9, 71, 73–5, 77, 80, 83, 86–7, 92, 94–5, 97, 99, 104, 110, 113, 116 (23 Sept. 1291), 117, 121–7, 129, 130.

William of BARDWELL was a juror for the double hundred in 1285 (*Suffolk Hundred*, xix).

Richard of BARNHAM held movables assessed at £2 3s 9d in Ixworth Thorpe in 1283 and with Simon of Gislingham appeared as a juror at the inquisition *post*

date the change to the years 1291 to 1294 (*Carte Nativorum: A Peterborough Abbey Cartulary of the Fourteenth Century*, ed. C.N.L. Brooke and M.M. Postan, Northamptonshire Record Society, 20 (1960), xvii and nn). Elizabeth Rutledge noticed the same effect on the deeds enrolled in Norwich at this time, commenting that where the *tenendum* clause in fee simple occasionally made reference to the grantor she had an example of 'outdated conveyancing' practice ('Property transfer and enrolment in Norwich 1285–1311', in *Men of Property: an Analysis of the Norwich Enrolled Deeds 1285–1311*, ed. U. Priestley, Norwich 1983, 41–69 (at 58–9)).

104 See above, pp. 21–2.

mortem of Euphemia Comyn of Fakenham in 1288/9 (*Suffolk Hundred*, t. 31; 90). He witnessed nos 10, 13, 15, 19, 25, 27–9, 35–6, 45, 76, 94, 107, 110, 121, and appeared in 2 (as grantee), 3 (as grantee), 90 (as grantor), 94 , 107, 108 (as grantor), 123 (as grantor), 169 (7 Nov. 1315, by which time he was dead).

Sir Eustace of BARNINGHAM appeared in the return of 1280 as the chief lord of Barningham with extensive lands and rents in the vill. In 1283, he had movables assessed at £9 3s 6d in Barningham (*Suffolk Hundred*, 28, 30, 31, 78; t. 6).

Thomas son of BARTHOLOMEW appeared in the 1280 return holding 2 roods of arable land in Coney Weston (*Suffolk Hundred*, 25).

Robert of BLACKBOROUGH held movables assessed at £2 19s 9d in Ixworth in 1283 and in 1285 was a juror for the double hundred (*Suffolk Hundred*, t. 17; xix). He witnessed nos 8, 13, 16–17, 20–2, 25, 27, 31, 34–6, 45, 57, 73, 99, 106, 108.

Richard de BOYLAND was dead by 4 Oct. 1296. His heir was his son John aged twenty-two and more (*CIPM*, iii, n. 365; *Cal. Genealogicum*, 524–5).

Robert de BRAKEBREGH held movables assessed at £2 19s 9d in Ixworth in 1283 (*Suffolk Hundred*, t. 17). He witnessed nos 10 (10 Nov. 1282), 19, 32, 55.

Cecily of BRAKELOND held movables assessed at £2 11s 3d in Bardwell in 1283 (*Suffolk Hundred*, t. 3). She appeared in charters 90, 115 (as co-grantor), 126 (as co-grantor).

William BRETON appeared in the return of 1280 holding in Stanton of Clavering hundred (Norfolk) an acre of land for an eighteenth part of the suit of the hundred (*Suffolk Hundred*, 57) and he appeared in 1284/5 (Rye, *FF Suffolk*, 86). He witnessed nos 40, 42, 44, 50, 52, 65, 70, 100 and appeared in 114 (as grantor).

Ralph CASSAMERRE appeared on 18 September 1292 (*Pinchbeck*, i, 59). He appeared in no. 74.

Walter the CHAPLAIN (alias Walter le SIRE) of Ixworth Thorpe in 1283 held movables assessed at 12s 6d in Ixworth Thorpe (*Suffolk Hundred*, t. 31) and £1 12s 9d in Walsham le Willows (*Suffolk Hundred*, t. 33). He appeared in nos 85, 110 (as grantor), 111, 121 (as grantor), 125.

Sir William de CRIKETOT, son of Sir William de Criketot, entered into his inheritance in March 1269 aged thirty-one years and more (*Cal. Genealogicum*, 135; *CIPM*, i, nos 704, 705; *Ex. Rot. Fin.*, ii, 410, 485); he appeared in 1272/3 and 1281/2 (Rye, *FF Suffolk*, 114, 137); he appeared in the return of 1280 as the chief lord of Great Ashfield and of Ashfield and in 1283, he had movables assessed at £43 5s 6½d in Great Ashfield and £6 13s 6d in Ixworth making him the second most heavily assessed lay man in the hundred after Sir William of Pakenham (*Suffolk Hundred*, xx, 5–8, 86; tt. 1, 17). Sir William died on 1 May 1299 when his heir was found to be his son William aged twenty-three years and more (*Cal. Genealogicum*, 570; *CIPM*, iii, n. 537). He witnessed no. 27 and appeared in nos 61 (as grantor), 178 (as grantor). His son witnessed nos 5 (6 Oct. 1304), 6 (7 Nov. 1304) and appeared in no. 131 (7 Nov. 1304).

Robert DISPENSER held movables assessed at £1 11s 6d in Ixworth in 1283

(*Suffolk Hundred*, t. 17). He witnessed charter 57 and appeared in 27, 30, 121, 130.

Walter DISPENSER held movables assessed at £3 1s 3d in 1283 in Bardwell (*Suffolk Hundred*, t. 4). He witnessed nos 10 (10 Nov. 1282), 11 (11 Jan. 1283), 13, 14 (9 July 1282), 15, 32, 57, 107.

Aluered of DRINKSTONE held movables assessed at £1 10s 0d in Bardwell in 1283 (*Suffolk Hundred*, t. 4).

Robert of DRINKSTONE held movables assessed at £1 2s 6d in Bardwell in 1283 (*Suffolk Hundred*, t. 4) and appeared in 1304/5 (Rye, *FF Suffolk*, 108). He witnessed nos 4, 7, 9 (16 March 1281), 14 (9 July 1282), 15, 20, 27, 39, 57, 58–60, 78 (7 Dec. 1280), 80, 83, 126, 128 and appeared in 22 (as grantor), 23 (22 April 1305 as grantor), 24 (15 Dec. 1293 as grantee), 87.

Robert ENGINEER (Gynour/Engynour) appeared in the return of 1280 holding a messuage and extensive lands in Market Weston, a messuage and extensive lands in Knettishall (*Suffolk Hundred*, 28, 45, 88); he held movables assessed at £16 12s 10d in Market Weston in 1283 and in 1285 he was a juror for the double hundred (*Suffolk Hundred*, t. 22; xix). He appeared on 18 September 1292 (*Pinchbeck*, i, 59). He witnessed nos 53 (26 May 1296), 54 (30 Aug. 1294), 60.

Alice, wife of Paulyn FELOUN, held movables assessed at £1 13s 2d in Ixworth Thorpe in 1283 (*Suffolk Hundred*, t. 31).

John of GEDDING appeared in 1261/2, 1273/4, 1297/8, 1308/9 (Rye, *FF Suffolk*, 63, 75, 102, 117) and in May 1307 (*CIPM*, iv, n. 435 (319)).

GEOFFREY the marshal appeared in the return of 1280 holding 8 acres of land in Walsham le Willows, a messuage and 40 acres of land in Rickinghall, 8 acres and certain rents in Troston; he held movables assessed at £5 11s 3d in Troston in 1283; and in 1285 was a juror for the double hundred (*Suffolk Hundred*, 12, 26, 38, 39; t. 32; xix). He witnessed nos 8, 41 (28 April 1271), 47, 63, 68, 90, 106 and appeared in 98 (as grantor), 130 (as grantor).

Simon of GISLINGHAM was mentioned in 1275/6 (Rye, *FF Suffolk*, 77); on 21 Sept. 1279 he and his associates were summoned as defendants in a case concerning trespass (*Cal. Patent Rolls, 1272–81*, 348); he held rents in Stowlangtoft in 1280; he held movables assessed at £2 1s 10d in Ixworth Thorpe in 1283 and in 1288/9 with Richard of Barnham he was a juror at the inquisition *post mortem* of Euphemia Comyn of Fakenham (*Suffolk Hundred*, 19; t. 31; 90). He died sometime before 1303/4 (Rye, *FF Suffolk*, 107). He witnessed nos 9 (16 March 1281), 17, 19, 20, 24 (15 Dec. 1293), 45, 53 (26 May 1296), 55–8, 61, 69, 71, 74–5, 80, 86–7, 90, 99, 107–8, 113, 124–5, 128–9; he appeared in 7, 15, 20, 25 (as grantor), 26 (24 Nov. 1294 as grantor), 27–8 (as grantor), 29–30 (as grantee), 31–2 (as grantor), 33 (10 Nov. 1282 as grantor), 34–6 (as grantor), 69, 73, 83, 97, 116 (23 Sept. 1291), 169, 178 (as grantee).

Matilda de la GRENE held movables assessed at £3 5s 4d in Ixworth in 1283 (*Suffolk Hundred*, t. 17).

Hubert HAKUN appeared in 1252 (*CIPM*, i, n. 258).

HENRY the tailor (Cyssor) held movables assessed at £3 15s 0d in Ixworth in 1283 (*Suffolk Hundred*, t. 17).

John HEREWARD held movables assessed at £1 12s 3d in Ixworth Thorpe in 1283 (*Suffolk Hundred*, t. 31).

Walter of HERTFORD appeared in the return of 1280 holding a messuage and extensive lands in Bardwell (*Suffolk Hundred*, 32 (5)). He witnessed nos 9 (16 March 1281), 18, 37, 43–4, 50, 70, 109.

Robert de le HILL of Bardwell witnessed nos 1 (6 Oct. 1314), 82 (21 Nov. 1307), 134 (27 Feb. 1311), 136 (1 May 1309), 141 (12 May 1311), 143 (12 May 1311), 144 (12 May 1311), 146 (27 July 1310), 149 (21 Nov. 1307), 155 (25 July 1310), 159 (8 July 1307), 162 (1 May 1311), 163 (7 May 1307), 164 (1 May 1309), 165 (6 Nov. 1313), 171 (24 June 1315).

Alexander HUBERT held movables assessed at £1 1s 3d in Ixworth Thorpe in 1283 (*Suffolk Hundred*, t. 31).

Alice, daughter of Geoffrey HUBERT, held movables assessed at £2 14s 9d in Ixworth Thorpe in 1283 (*Suffolk Hundred*, t. 31). She appeared as the grantor in charters 7, 8, 10 (10 Nov. 1282), 11 (11 Jan. 1283), 12 (15 June 1281), 13, 14 (9 July 1282), 15.

Adam of INGHAM appeared in the return of 1280 holding rents in Bardwell and 340 acres of arable land, 2½ acres of meadow, and 33 acres of pasture in Ingham. In 1283, he held movables assessed at £2 3s 8d in Ingham (*Suffolk Hundred*, 33, 36, 85; t. 16). His son, Salomon, entered into his inheritance between 1283 and 1286 (*Suffolk Hundred*, 33, 36, 85; t. 16).

Salomon of INGHAM, son of Adam and Laetitia Ingham, entered in to his father's inheritance before 1285/6. In 1280 Adam appeared in the return holding rents in Bardwell and 340 acres of arable land, 2½ acres of meadow, and 33 acres of pasture in Ingham. In 1283, he held movables assessed at £2 3s 8d in Ingham (*Suffolk Hundred*, 33, 36, 85; t. 16).

Geoffrey son of JOHN appeared in the return of 1280 holding 3 roods of land in Stanton and in 1283, he held movables assessed at £2 12s 0d in the same vill (*Suffolk Hundred*, 55; t. 27).

Walter KENNE appeared in the return of 1280 holding half an acre of land in Stanton. In 1283 he held movables assessed at £2 10s 0d in the same vill, where he was styled 'capellanus', and £3 12s 3d in Ixworth Thorpe (*Suffolk Hundred*, 50, 90; tt. 27, 31). He witnessed nos 22, 23 (22 April 1305), 24 (15 Dec. 1293), 71, 72 (12 March 1310), 75, 79 (8 Jan. 1307), 118 (12 March 1309), 119 (10 April 1309), 120 (9 March 1309), 132 (9 Feb. 1309), 134 (27 Feb. 1311), 135, 136 (1 May 1309), 137 (23 July 1310), 138 (16 July 1310), 139 (23 Nov. 1307), 140 (4 April 1310), 141 (12 May 1311), 142 (11 June 1300), 143 (12 May 1311), 144 (12 May 1311), 145 (2 Aug. 1310), 146 (27 July 1310), 147 (6 March 1309), 149 (21 Nov. 1307), 150 (4 April 1310), 151 (17 July 1310), 152 (27 July 1310), 154 (25 Jan. 1312), 155 (25 July 1310), 157 (3 March 1311), 161 (26 May 1311), 162 (1 May 1311), 164 (1 May 1309), and appeared in 32, 55 (as grantor), 56 (as grantor), 72, 93 (16 June 1307 as grantee), 118, 152, 156 (24 Aug. 1310 as grantor), 158 (23 Aug. 1310 exchange), 159 (8 July 1307 as grantor), 160 (25 Aug. 1307 as grantor), 166.

William KENNE held movables assessed at £1 1s 3d in Ixworth Thorpe in 1283 (*Suffolk Hundred*, t. 31), and was mentioned in 1320/1 (Rye, *FF Suffolk*, 147). He witnessed nos 147 (6 March 1309), 162 (1 May 1311), 165 (6 Nov. 1313), 169 (7 Nov. 1315), and appeared in 148 (13 May 1312 in an agreement), 158

(23 Aug. 1310 in an agreement), 163 (7 May 1307 as grantor), 170 (in an agreement), 171 (24 June 1315 as grantor), 173 (10 June 1319 in an agreement), 174 (7 Feb. 1317 in an agreement), 175 (10 June 1319 as grantor).

Geoffrey LEWIN held movables assessed at £5 7s 6d in Ixworth Thorpe in 1283 (*Suffolk Hundred*, t. 31).

John LEWIN held movables assessed at 11s 3d in Ixworth Thorpe in 1283 (*Suffolk Hundred*, t. 31). He witnessed nos 17, 19–20, 31, 71, 72 (12 March 1310), 137 (23 July 1310), 138 (16 July 1310), 142 (11 June 1300), 146 (27 July 1310), 149 (21 Nov. 1307), 152 (27 July 1310), 155 (25 July 1310), 157 (3 March 1311), 164 (1 May 1309), and appeared in 83 (as grantor), 116 (23 Sept. 1291 as grantor), 128 (as grantor), 133, 159 (8 July 1307 as co-grantor), 160 (25 Aug. 1307 as co-grantor), 166.

William I LEWIN witnessed nos 38, 41 (28 April 1271), and appeared in 85.

Bartholomew of LIVERMERE, son of Henry of Little Livermere, appeared in the return of 1280 holding a messuage and extensive lands in Little Livermere. He held movables assessed at £7 2s 6d in the same vill in 1283 and in 1285 he was a juror for the double hundred (*Suffolk Hundred*, 40; t. 21; xix). He witnessed nos 56, 124, 156 (24 Aug. 1310), 158 (23 Aug. 1310), 169 (7 Nov. 1315), 171 (24 June 1315).

Henry of LIVERMERE appeared in 1268/9 (Rye, *FF Suffolk*, 63) and seems to have died before 1280 (*Suffolk Hundred*, 40).

John of LIVERMERE appeared in 1291/2 (Rye, *FF Suffolk*, 95). He witnessed nos 4, 38, 49, 66, 67.

John le MAN held movables assessed at £2 16s 6d in Honington in 1283 (*Suffolk Hundred*, t. 13).

Matilda le MAYSTER held movables assessed at 7s 8d in Ixworth Thorpe in 1283 (*Suffolk Hundred*, t. 31).

Giles of NECTON, son of Sir William of Necton, appeared in 1272/3 (Rye, *FF Suffolk*, 75). In September 1281, his betrothal to Sibyl de Beauchamp was mentioned (*CIPM*, ii, n. 409). He held movables assessed at £11 2s 6d in Hepworth in 1283 (*Suffolk Hundred*, t. 11) and was dead by 1300 when his heir William was holding in Saxham (*Pinchbeck*, i, 284).

Sir William of NECTON appeared in 1257/8, 1268/9, 1272/3, and 1274/5 (Rye, *FF Suffolk*, 59, 68, 75, 77). In 1262/3, he was forty years old when he succeeded to the lands of his father, Henry of Necton (*Cal. Genealogicum*, 104; *Ex Rot. Fin.*, ii, 398). He appeared in the return of 1280 holding rents in Barningham (*Suffolk Hundred*, 29, 30, 53, 54), and 3 roods and 5½ acres of land in Stanton. He appeared in the inquisition *post mortem* of Roger de Beauchamp in September 1281 (*CIPM*, ii, n. 409). He witnessed charter 96 and appeared in 46 (as grantee), 64 (as grantee).

Henry son of NICHOLAS of St Edmunds appeared in 1280 (*Suffolk Hundred*, 77). He held movables assessed at £18 15s 6d in Bardwell in 1283 (*Suffolk Hundred*, t. 3). He appeared in 1290–3 (*State Trials*, 67–70).

Henry son of NICHOLAS appeared in the return of 1280 holding rents in Langham, and lands in Stanton (*Suffolk Hundred*, 6, 52, 54, 56, 60, 61).

John OSSELYN (Oscelyn/Ocelin) appeared in the return of 1280 holding 21 acres of land in Stanton and in 1283 he held movables assessed at £2 10s 0d in the same vill (*Suffolk Hundred*, 48, 55; t. 28).

Mr John of PAKENHAM was dead by 1280 (*Suffolk Hundred*, 33, 44). He occurs in 1260/1, 1262/3, 1268/9 and 1269/70 (Rye, *FF Suffolk*, 63–4, 68–9, 71; Rye, *FF Norfolk*, 109). He appeared in charters 4, 43, 111.

John of PAKENHAM witnessed nos 6 (7 Nov. 1304), 37, 39, 43–4, 50, 63, 70, 85, 111.

Thomas of PAKENHAM was a younger son of William of Pakenham. When Edmund, William's elder son, entered into his inheritance in 1305 he was described as twenty-seven years or more, making Thomas no more than twenty-six in 1305 (*Cal. Genealogicum*, 684).

Sir William of PAKENHAM was dead by 7 November 1304 (nos 6, 131), though his death was not notified to the escheator until 22 Jan. 1305 (*Cal. Fine Rolls*, i, 507).

Thomas le PALMER held movables assessed at £2 4s 3d in Knettishall and £5 5s 4d in West Stow in 1283 (*Suffolk Hundred*, tt. 19, 36).

Sir Reginald PECCHE appeared in 1268/9 and 1269/70 (Rye, *FF Suffolk*, 69, 71). He appeared in the return of 1280 as the chief lord of Stowlangtoft and holding certain rents in Troston, and in 1283 he held movables assessed at £16 in Stowlangtoft. In 1285 Sir Reginald was a juror for the double hundred (*Suffolk Hundred*, 13–19, 38, 90, xix; t. 29). In autumn 1298, Sir Reginald was a witness in the proof of age of William son and heir of John the Marshal when he was described as being aged fifty with a son, Geoffrey, to be aged twenty-two on the feast of St Gregory (12 March) 1299 (*CIPM*, iii, n. 483). Geoffrey entered into his inheritance in 1303 (*Suffolk Hundred*, 90). He witnessed nos 27, 30, 53 (26 May 1296), 54 (30 Aug. 1294), 55, 61, 80, 89, 96, 129.

Robert PUTTOCK appeared in the return of 1280 holding a messuage, 2 acres of arable land and 5 roods of meadow in Ixworth Thorpe (*Suffolk Hundred*, 44).

Geoffrey son of RALPH held movables assessed at £2 15s 0d in Hopton in 1283 (*Suffolk Hundred*, t. 14). He witnessed nos 45, 137 (23 July 1310), 138 (16 July 1310), 139 (23 Nov. 1307), 140 (4 April 1310), 142 (11 June 1300), 150 (4 April 1310), 151 (17 July 1310), 154 (25 Jan. 1312), 162 (1 May 1311), 163 (7 May 1307) and appeared in 1, 153 (19 March 1308, an agreement), 159 (8 July 1307 as co-grantor), 160 (25 Aug. 1307 as co-grantor), 166–7, 176 (3 Nov. 1318 as grantor).

John son of RALPH of Hepworth appeared in the return of 1280 holding 10 acres of land in Stanton (*Suffolk Hundred*, 47).

Robert son of RALPH witnessed nos 1 (6 Oct. 1314), 20, 22, 45, 56, 71, 72 (12 March 1310), 73, 79 (8 Jan. 1307), 86, 101 (8 July 1305), 128–9, 132 (9 Feb. 1309), 135, 137 (23 July 1310), 138 (16 July 1310), 139 (23 Nov. 1307), 140 (4 April 1310), 142 (11 June 1300), 143 (12 May 1311), 147 (6 March 1309), 148 (13 May 1312), 149 (21 Nov. 1307), 150 (4 April 1310), 151 (17 July 1310), 152 (27 July 1310), 154 (25 Jan. 1312), 155 (25 July 1310), 156 (24 Aug. 1310), 157 (3 March 1311), 158 (23 Aug. 1310), 161 (26 May 1311), 162 (1 May 1311), 163 (7 May 1307) and appeared in 120 (9 March 1309), 136 (1 May 1309 as grantor), 137, 145 (2 Aug. 1310 as grantor), 146 (27 July 1310 as grantee), 153 (19 March 1308, an agreement), 159 (8 July 1307 as co-grantor), 160 (25 Aug. 1307 as co-grantor), 164 (1 May 1309 as grantor), 165 (6 Nov. 1313 as grantor), 166 (as grantor).

Thomas REVEL witnessed nos 8, 17, 19–20, 28, 31, 51 (17 Feb. 1290), 55, 61, 68, 125, 128.

Robert of RICKINGHALL witnessed nos 4, 7–8, 9 (16 March 1281), 11 (11 Jan. 1283), 13, 14 (9 July 1282), 15, 34, 74, 76, 107.

William son of ROBERT of Bardwell was dead by 1280 when his widow was in receipt of 4s 11d of rent in Bardwell (*Suffolk Hundred*, 31). He witnessed nos 4, 18, 37–8, 42, 43–4, 50, 52, 62, 70, 84–5, 88, 91, 109, 111 and appeared in 18.

Nicholas ROBYN appeared in the return of 1280 holding 12 acres of arable land in common and an acre of land in Troston; he held movables assessed at £11 3s 9d in Troston in 1283; and appeared as a juror for the double hundred in 1285 (*Suffolk Hundred*, 38, 39; t. 32; xix). He witnessed nos 8, 32, 36, 57, 68, 97, 106 and appeared in 80 (as grantor).

Matilda le ROS appeared in 1268/9 (Rye, *FF Suffolk*, 71).

Richard le ROS appeared in the return of 1280 holding rent in Bardwell (*Suffolk Hundred*, 32).

William son of Nicholas le ROS appeared in 1285/6 (Rye, *FF Suffolk*, 87).

John SCOT was killed in a hunting accident in 1286 (*Suffolk Hundred*, 83).

Robert of SHELLAND appeared in the return of 1280 holding a cottage in Stanton (*Suffolk Hundred*, 48).

Alexander of STANTON, brother of Nicholas of Stanton, appeared in the return of 1280 holding 15 acres of land and 3 acres of pasture in Stanton (*Suffolk Hundred*, 59). He witnessed nos 5 (6 Oct. 1304), 6 (7 Nov. 1304), 17, 19–22, 28–9, 51 (17 Feb. 1290), 55, 61, 80, 89 and appeared in 133 (3 Nov. 1294 as grantee).

John of STANTON was mentioned in 1264 and appeared in the return of 1280 holding a share of a messuage and lands in Stowlangtoft (*Suffolk Hundred*, 16, 78). He witnessed nos 37, 44, 50, 63, 66–7, 70, 102, 114.

Nicholas of STANTON appeared in the return of 1280 holding rents in Knettishall, and lands and rents in Stanton. In 1283, he held movables assessed at £8 12s 0d in Stanton (*Suffolk Hundred*, 46–7, 50, 58, 59; t. 27).

Thomas of STANTON appeared in the return of 1280. In 1283, he held movables assessed at £1 12s 4d in Barnham (*Suffolk Hundred*, 48; t. 5). He witnessed nos 37, 42, 48, 62, 65, 70, 84, 102, 103, 114.

Adam de SUTHENTON witnessed nos 4, 18, 38, 42, 43–4, 65–7, 70, 85, 91.

Richard de SUTHENTON appeared in the return of 1280 holding a messuage in Barningham and 1½ acres of arable land in Stowlangtoft; his widow was assessed on her movables there to the value of £1 13s 2d in 1283 (*Suffolk Hundred*, 19, 31; t. 29 – she appears as Olyva relict of Richard). He witnessed nos 8, 10 (10 Nov. 1282), 13, 28, 30, 32, 33 (10 Nov. 1282), 36, 57–61, 68, 74, 76–7, 78 (7 Dec. 1280), 92, 94, 97, 108, 113, 121–2.

Ralph SYMOND held movables assessed at £3 12s 3d in Ixworth Thorpe in 1283 (*Suffolk Hundred*, t. 31). He witnessed nos 16, 29, 32, 76 and appeared in 74.

John le SYRE the elder held movables assessed at 14s 9d in Ixworth Thorpe in 1283 (*Suffolk Hundred*, t. 31). He witnessed nos 10 (10 Nov. 1282), 11 (11 Jan. 1283), 16–22, 29, 34–5, 71, 90, 123 and appeared in 8, 34, 68, 99, 101 (8 July 1305 as grantor), 139 (23 Nov. 1307), 160 (25 Aug. 1307 as co-grantor), 162 (1 May 1311), 166, 172.

Nicholas le SYRE witnessed nos 72 (12 March 1310), 145 (2 Aug. 1310), 149 (21 Nov. 1307), 152 (27 July 1310), 161 (26 May 1311), 164 (1 May 1309) and appeared in 129 (8 July 1305 as co-grantor), 148 (13 May 1312), 159 (8 July 1307 as co-grantor), 160 (25 Aug. 1307 as co-grantor), 166, 172 (as grantor).

Robert le SYRE appeared in the return of 1280 holding 30d of rent in Stowlangtoft (*Suffolk Hundred*, 18), and in 1283 the Sire movables in Ixworth Thorpe were assessed at £3 2s 0d and £1 19s 4d (*Suffolk Hundred*, t. 31). He witnessed nos 7, 9 (16 March 1281), 10 (10 Nov. 1282), 11 (11 Jan. 1283), 12 (15 June 1281), 13, 14 (9 July 1282), 15, 17–19, 21, 24 (15 Dec. 1293), 27–31, 33 (10 Nov. 1282), 35, 58, 138 and appeared in 71, 97.

William le SYRE appeared in the return of 1280 holding rent in Troston and 3 acres of land in Ixworth Thorpe (*Suffolk Hundred*, 39, 44) and in 1283 the Sire movables in Ixworth Thorpe were assessed at £3 2s 0d and £1 19s 4d (*Suffolk Hundred*, t. 31).

William son of William le SYRE appeared in 1303/4 (Rye, *FF Suffolk*, 107).

Thomas THEDRED was dead by 1280 (*Suffolk Hundred*, 31).

Matthew of THELNETHAM occurs in 1238/9 as the heir of Peter of Thelnetham, and in 1257/8, 1259/60, 1268/9 and 1283/4 (Rye, *FF Suffolk*, 40, 59, 63, 68, 185). He appeared in the return of 1280 having donated to the chamberlain (*camerarius*) of St Edmunds 3s of rent in Troston and he acted as a juror for the double hundred in 1285 (*Suffolk Hundred*, 38, xix). He witnessed nos 4, 39, 41 (28 April 1271), 46, 49, 53 (26 May 1296), 54 (30 Aug. 1294), 62, 66–7, 102–3, 156 (24 Aug. 1310), 158 (23 Aug. 1310) and appeared in 63 (as grantor).

Sir Peter of THELNETHAM appeared in the return of 1280 holding extensive lands and rents in Hopton, Barningham, Barnham, Troston, Little Livermere, and Knettishall. He held movables assessed at £40 in Thelnetham in 1283, making him the third highest assessed layman in Blackbourn hundred after Sir William of Pakenham and Sir William de Criketot (*Suffolk Hundred*, xx, 27, 31, 36–9, 41, 45; t. 30). Sir Peter was mentioned in a commission of *oyer et terminer* on 27 December 1285 touching an appeal in which Edmund de St Claro accused Peter, Baldwin Maneres and others of robbery and burning down his house at Thelnetham (*Cal. Patent Rolls, 1281–92*, 200). He witnessed nos 5 (6 Oct. 1304), 6 (7 Nov. 1304), 22, 31, 56, 71, 82 (21 Nov. 1307), 96, 101 (8 July 1305), 117, 118 (12 March 1309), 119 (10 April 1309), 120 (9 March 1309), 124, 135, 136 (1 May 1309), 147 (6 March 1309), 152 (27 July 1310), 153 (19 March 1308), 158 (23 Aug. 1310), 159 (8 July 1307).

William of THELNETHAM appeared in the return of 1280 holding a messuage and extensive lands in Troston; held movables assessed at £12 11s 0d in Troston and £3 14s 2d in Barnham in 1283; and was a juror for the double hundred in 1285 (*Suffolk Hundred*, 38, 91; tt. 4, 32; xix). He appeared on 18 September 1292 (*Pinchbeck*, i, 59). He witnessed nos 5 (6 Oct. 1304), 6 (7 Nov. 1304), 7–8, 13, 15, 21, 25, 29, 31, 34–6, 39, 41 (28 April 1271), 45–7, 51 (17 Feb. 1290), 55–61, 63–4, 69, 74, 76–7, 87, 89–90, 94–5, 98–9, 104, 106, 108, 110, 113, 116 (23 Sept. 1291), 117, 121, 123–4, 127, 129–30 and appeared in 68 (as grantor), 97 (as grantor).

Richard son of THOMAS appeared in the return of 1280 holding a messuage and lands in Stanton and in 1283, he held movables assessed at 15s 0d in the same vill (*Suffolk Hundred*, 52, 55, 57, 59; t. 28).

Geoffrey of THORPE appeared in 1246/7 and was dead by 1263 when his widow, Margaret, was in a suit against Mr John of Pakenham (Rye, *FF Suffolk*, 48, 64). He witnessed nos 18, 37, 62, 84–5, 105, 109 and he appeared in 38, 40 (as grantor), 42 (as grantor), 43–4 (as grantor), 45, 48–50 (as grantor), 51, 52 (as grantor), 65 (as grantor), 66–7, 74.

Margaret, widow of Geoffrey of THORPE, appeared as a widow in 1262/3 (Rye, *FF Suffolk*, 64). She appeared in nos 39 (as grantor), 92.

John of THORPE held movables assessed at £1 12s 0d in Ixworth in 1283 (*Suffolk Hundred*, t. 17). He appeared in nos 38 (as grantor), 46 (as grantor), 63, 67 (as grantor).

The heirs of John of THORPE appeared in the return of 1280 holding a messsuage and 6 acres of land from the abbot of St Edmunds in Ashfield (*Suffolk Hundred*, 8).

Nicholas of TROSTON, chaplain, held movables assessed at £6 7s 6d in Troston in 1283 (*Suffolk Hundred*, t. 32).

Robert ULTRA AQUAM appeared in 1268/9 (Rye, *FF Suffolk*, 67); he appeared in the return of 1280 holding 14d of rents in Ixworth, a messuage and extensive lands in Bardwell; he held movables assessed at £9 19s 6d in Bardwell in 1283, and he was a juror for the double hundred in 1285 (*Suffolk Hundred*, 13, 31, 32, xix; t. 4). He witnessed nos 7–8, 9 (16 March 1281), 10 (10 Nov. 1282), 11 (11 Jan. 1283), 12 (15 June 1281), 13, 14 (9 July 1282), 15, 17–21, 24 (15 Dec. 1293), 25, 28, 32, 33 (10 Nov. 1282), 34–6, 38–9, 43–5, 47–8, 55–60, 68, 70–1, 74–6, 78 (7 Dec. 1280), 86, 88, 90, 92, 94–5, 98–9, 104, 106–8, 110, 113, 117, 121, 123, 125, 129–30 and appeared in 48, 85, 87, 100 (as grantor).

John de VERDUN appeared in the return of 1280 holding freely in Troston 43 acres of arable land and 13 acres of heath with the right to have a fold (*Suffolk Hundred*, 38).

Adam of WALPOLE occurs in 1274/5 and 1277/8 (Rye, *FF Suffolk*, 77, 126).

Sir Roger of WALSHAM held movables assessed at £6 2s 1d in Walsham le Willows in 1283. In 1285, he was a juror for the double hundred. Sir Roger was dead by 1289/90 (*Suffolk Hundred*, pp. xix, 91; t. 33).

William le WARDE witnessed nos 22, 23 (22 April 1305), 27–9, 31, 55, 61, 71, 73, 75, 118 (12 March 1309), 122, 128, 140 (4 April 1310), 145 (2 Aug. 1310), 146 (27 July 1310), 148 (13 May 1312), 150 (4 April 1310), 164 (1 May 1309) and appeared in 1 (6 Oct. 1314 as grantor), 17 (as grantor), 19–21 (as grantor), 35, 72 (12 March 1310 as grantor), 82 (21 Nov. 1307 as grantor), 89, 120 (9 March 1309 as grantor), 137 (23 July 1310 as grantor), 138 (16 July 1310), 139 (23 Nov. 1307), 149 (21 Nov. 1307 as grantor), 151 (17 July 1310 as grantor), 157 (3 March 1311 as grantor), 160 (25 Aug. 1307 as co-grantor), 162 (1 May 1311 as grantor), 166, 167 (as grantor).

Berard of WATTISFIELD with Sir John de St Clare was a juryman for the liberty of St Edmunds in 1275 (*Suffolk Hundred*, 93).

John son of WILLIAM of Bardwell appeared in the return of 1280 holding a messuage and 8 acres of arable land in Bardwell, a messuage and an acre of land in Stanton, a share of a penny of rent in Stanton and rent in Langham

(*Suffolk Hundred*, 6, 31, 51, 60); and he held movables assessed at 9s 0d in Bardwell and £2 15s ½d in Sapiston in 1283 (*Suffolk Hundred*, tt. 4, 26). He witnessed nos 8, 9 (16 March 1281), 10 (10 Nov. 1282), 11 (11 Jan. 1283), 12 (15 June 1281), 14 (9 July 1282), 17, 19, 23 (22 April 1305), 24 (15 Dec. 1293), 25, 27–8, 31–2, 33 (10 Nov. 1282), 34–5, 41 (28 April 1271), 45, 48, 54 (30 Aug. 1294), 56, 61, 68, 71, 73, 75–6, 78 (7 Dec. 1280), 83, 86, 92, 95, 97, 98, 101 (8 July 1305), 110, 113, 116 (23 Sept. 1291), 117, 121–7, 155 (25 July 1310) and appeared in 57–9 (agreements), 60 (as grantor), 79 (8 Jan. 1307 an agreement), 95, 155 (25 July 1310).

Robert son of WILLIAM of Rickinghall held movables assessed at £4 12s 6d in Bardwell in 1283 (*Suffolk Hundred*, t. 4).

William of WILLINGHAM appeared in the return of 1280 holding 2 acres of arable land in Troston and he held movables assessed at £4 8s 6d in 1283 in the same vill (*Suffolk Hundred*, 39; t. 32). He witnessed nos 9 (16 March 1281), 10 (10 Nov. 1282), 12 (15 June 1281), 21, 33 (10 Nov. 1282), 57, 68, 78 (7 Dec. 1280), 94 , 106, 108, 117, 130 and appeared in 33 (10 Nov. 1282), 35, 74 (as grantor), 122 (as grantor), 129 (as grantor), 141 (as grantor).

Richard de WYKES appeared with his wife Johanna in 1271/2 (Rye, *FF Suffolk*, 73) and was dead by 1280 when his heir appeared in the return holding 4 acres of land in Stowlangtoft (*Suffolk Hundred*, 18). He witnessed nos 41 (28 April 1271), 63 and appeared in 50.

Richard de WYKES witnessed nos 79 (8 Jan. 1307), 93 (16 June 1307), 118 (12 March 1309), 119 (10 April 1309), 141 (12 May 1311), 143 (12 May 1311), 144 (12 May 1311), 153 (19 March 1308), 159 (8 July 1307).

BL CAMPBELL CHARTERS XVII

1. [*fo. 1r*] Grant in heredity by William le Warde of Ixworth Thorpe to Thomas of Pakenham and his wife, Alice, their heirs and assigns, for a certain sum of money in cash, of a parcel of arable land with appurtenances situated in the field of Ixworth Thorpe called *Wardishamus toft* between the land of Geoffrey son of Ralph on the one side and the land of Emma Coctoyn on the other, of which one headland abuts on the land of the said Thomas and the other on that of the grantor, to have and to hold with appurtenances of the capital lord of the fee by due and customary service. Warranty is granted against all persons in perpetuity. Sealed in witness.
[Hiis] Testibus: Willelmo de Langham, Roberto Balhernd, Roberto le Mayster, Roberto filio Radulfi, Roberto de le Hil et aliis.

Ixworth Thorpe, 6 Oct. 1314

2. Quitclaim by John Aveney of Wangford (*Wannforth*) to Richard of Barnham (*Bernham*) of Ixworth Thorpe, for 5 marks of silver in cash, of all right that he has in an annual rent of 4s of silver which Richard paid him for the tenement which he held of him in the vill of Ixworth Thorpe with reliefs, wardships, escheats, and with all appurtenances which might come to John or his heirs, so that henceforth neither *dominus* John nor his heirs nor anyone in their name may have any right or legal claim in the said rent of 4s of silver for all reliefs, etc. In witness, etc.

[Mid – late thirteenth century]

3. Quitclaim by John Aveney of Wangford (*Wannforthe*) for himself and his heirs to Richard of Barnham (*Bernham*) of Ixworth Thorpe, his heirs and assigns, of all suit of court that he rendered to John from the meadow of the tenement which he held of John in the vill of Ixworth Thorpe, so that neither John nor his heirs nor anyone in their name may henceforth demand or claim suit of court from the said tenement, and for this remission and quitclaim Richard gave John half a mark of silver in cash. In order that this quitclaim may remain valid and stable in perpetuity, John's seal has been affixed, etc.

[Mid–late thirteenth century]

4. [*fo. 1v*] Grant in heredity by Mr John of Pakenham, rector of the church of Hawkedon, to his nephews, the brothers John and William of Pakenham, for their homage and service, of all his lands and tenements which he holds in the vill of Ixworth Thorpe with all liberties and appurtenances, that is, homages, services, rents, reliefs, escheats and wardships, meadows, pastures, in roads and footpaths, in waters and in all things and places that pertain to the grantor in the vill, to have and to hold of the grantor and his heirs freely, quit, wholly, well and in peace, in fee and heredity perpetually, rendering therefrom annually to the grantor, for the whole of his life, £40 sterling at two annual terms, namely, £20 at Michaelmas and £20 at Easter, and after his death annually to his heirs £20 of service at Michaelmas, rendering therefrom annually for him and his heirs to the capital

lords of the fees due and customary service for all services, aids, and customs and demands. Warranty is granted against all persons. Sealed in witness.
Hiis testibus: domino Matheo de Thelnitham, domino Ricardo de Norton', Willelmo filio Roberti de Berdewell, Adam de Suthenton', Willelmo Syre de Thorp, Johanne de Lyvermere, Roberto de Rekynghal', Roberto camerario, Roberto de Drenkyston', Adam de Pring(?), et aliis.

[Mid thirteenth century, before 12 May 1259]

This charter presumably dates from before Sir William received his grant of free warren on 12 May 1259 (*Cal. Charter Rolls, 1257–1300*, 17).

5. Quitclaim by William son of *dominus* William of Pakenham, kt, to William his father, his heirs and assigns, of all right and claim and all actions which he had or might have in his father's manor in Ixworth Thorpe with all its appurtenances and liberties without any reservation or objection by William son of William, his heirs and his assigns, freely, quit, fully and by inheritance, so that henceforth neither William son of William nor his heirs nor anyone in his name may have any right or legal claim in the foresaid manor with all its appurtenances. Sealed in witness.
Hiis testibus: Willelmo de Creketot, Thoma de Norton', Willelmo de Thelnitham, Petro de Thelnitham, Alexandro de Walsham, Nicholao de Trows, Alberico de Wykes, Petro de Thorp', Alexandro de Stanton', Thoma le Walys, Willelmo Cokeman, Willelmo Therny, Gilberto Alwy et aliis.

Norton, 6 Oct. 1304

See nos 6 and 131.

6. Grant in heredity by Edmund of Pakenham, kt, to Thomas his brother, of the whole of his manor of Ixworth Thorpe with all its appurtenances and with everything which pertains to and is situated and owed in the manor without any reservation, except the lease that *dominus* William his father formerly purchased from *dominus* William de Creketot, kt,[a] to have and to hold of him and his heirs by Thomas [*fo. 2r*] and the heirs of his body lawfully begotten, freely, quit, peaceably and by inheritance, rendering therefrom annually to the capital lord of the fee on behalf of the grantor and his heirs due and customary service. Warranty is granted against all persons, and if it should happen that Thomas dies without an heir of his body lawfully begotten, then the manor with all its appurtenances should revert to the grantor and his heirs without objection and interference from anyone. And for this concession, donation and warranty, Thomas gave to the grantor one hundred marks sterling in cash. Sealed in witness.
Hiis testibus: Willelmo de Creketot, Alberico de Wykes, Thoma de Norton', magistro[b] Ricardo de Felmingham, magistro Ricardo de Schipham, Galfrido Pecche, Willelmo de Thelnitham,[c] Petro de Thelnitham,[c] Nicholao de Trows, Johanne de Pakynham, Petro de Thorp', Alexandro de Stanton', et aliis.

Norton, Saturday 7 Nov. 1304

The original charter exists as BL Harleian Charter 54 F 5, 247mm wide x 100mm, tag

remains but seal missing.
See nos 5 and 131.

a Died 1 May 1299 (*Cal. Geneaologicum*, ii, 570).
b supplied by the original.
c Welnetham in the original, though almost certainly wrongly.

7. Grant in heredity by Alice daughter of Geoffrey of Thorpe to *dominus* William of Pakenham, kt, for his service and 40s sterling in cash, of one and a half acres of arable land in the field of Ixworth Thorpe beside that of John Hereward, of which one headland abuts on the land of William and the other on that of Simon of Gislingham (*Gesselingham*), be there more or less, to hold and to have of the grantor and her heirs by the same William and his heirs or whosoever to whom he may wish to grant, sell or otherwise assign it, freely, quit, well, peaceably and by inheritance, rendering therefrom annually to the grantor and her heirs a clove at Easter for all aids and demands. Warranty is granted against all persons in perpetuity. Sealed in witness.
Hiis [testibus]: Willelmo de Thelnitham, Radulfo de Berdwell', Roberto ultra aquam, Roberto de Rekynghal', Waltero le Spenser, Roberto de Drenkyston, Radulfo filio Symonis, Willelmo filio Ade, Ricardo de Elynham, Roberto le Syre, Willelmo le Syre, Petro de Thorp', et aliis.

[Late thirteenth century, before 1290]

8. Grant in heredity by Alice daughter of Geoffrey of Thorpe (*Thorp'*) to *dominus* William of Pakenham, kt, for his service and 20s sterling which he gave to her in cash, of a rent of 21d a year, to be received at two annual [*fo. 2v*] terms, that is, half at Michaelmas and the other half at Easter, namely, from Matilda and Phyllis, daughters of Robert To, 2d for the messuage of Hubert de Angirhal, and from Alexander the cobbler (*sutor*) 4d for his messuage beside the messuage formerly of Peter Schanke, and from Matilda le Ros 2½d for the messuage formerly of Robert Ketil beside the messuage of John Hereward, and from Ralph son of Simon 1d for his messuage beside the messuage of John le Syre, and from Matilda de la Grene 1½d for her messuage beside the messuage of William Cleyngholf, and from the said William Cleyngholf 1½d for his messuage beside the messuage of the said Matilda, and from the heir of Paulyn Feloun 6d for his messuage beside the messuage of William Hubert, and from Simon Sterre 2½d for one piece in *Dedemor* beside the meadow of William, to have and to hold of the grantor and her heirs by William and his heirs with homages, reliefs, wardships, escheats, suit of court and everything else which pertains to each of the said rents, freely, quit, well, peaceably and by inheritance, rendering therefrom annually to the grantor and her heirs a clove at Easter for all services, aids, exactions and secular demands. Warranty is granted against all persons in perpetuity. Sealed in witness.
Hiis testibus: Willelmo de Thelnitham, Radulfo de Berdewell, Johanne filio Willelmi, Roberto ultra aquam, Roberto de Rekynghal', Roberto de Blakeberth, Willelmo de Elyngham, Nicholao Robyn, Galfrido le marechal, Ricardo de Suthenton, Thoma Revel, Petro de Thorpe, et aliis.

[Third quarter of thirteenth century, before 1283]

9. Grant in heredity by William son of Ralph Cassamerre of Ixworth Thorpe to *dominus* William of Pakenham, kt, for his service and for 30s sterling in cash, of one and a half acres of arable land in the field of Ixworth Thorpe between the lands of William on the one side, abutting at one headland on the embankment which is called *Thorpepond*, be there more or less, to have and to hold of the grantor and his heirs by William and his heirs or whosoever to whom he may wish to grant, sell or otherwise assign it, freely, quit, well, peaceably and by inheritance, rendering therefrom annually to the grantor and his heirs a clove at Easter for all services, aids and demands. Warranty is granted against all persons in perpetuity. Sealed in witness.
Hiis testibus: Radulfo de Berdewell, Johanne filio Willelmi, Roberto ultra aquam, Waltero de Herdforde, Roberto de Rekynghal', Roberto de Drenkynson, Radulfo filio Symonis, Willelmo filio Ade, Willelmo de Wilyngham, Symone de Gesselingham, Roberto le Syre, Willelmo le Syre, et aliis.

Ixworth Thorpe, Sunday 16 March 1281

10. Grant in heredity by Alice daughter of Geoffrey Hubert of Ixworth Thorpe to *dominus* William of Pakenham, kt, for his service and for 10s sterling in cash, of three acres of arable land in the field of Ixworth Thorpe called *Northolm* beside the land of William, abutting at one headland on the common pasture, be there more or less, to hold and to have of the grantor and her heirs by William and his heirs or [*fo. 3r*] whosoever to whom he may wish to grant, sell or otherwise assign it, freely, quit, well, peaceably and by inheritance, rendering therefrom annually to the grantor and her heirs a clove at Michaelmas for all services, aids, all manner of suit of court and demands. Warranty is granted against all persons in perpetuity. Sealed in witness.
Hiis testibus: Johanne filio Willelmi, Radulfo de Berdewell', Ricardo de Suthentun', Roberto ultra aquam, Waltero le Spenser, Roberto de Brakebergh', Radulfo filio Symonis, Roberto le Syre, Willelmo le Syre, Johanne le Syre, Ricardo de Bernham, Willelmo de Wilingham, et aliis.

Ixworth Thorpe, Tuesday 10 Nov. 1282

See no. 33.

11. Grant in heredity by Alice daughter of Geoffrey Hubert of Ixworth Thorpe to *dominus* William of Pakenham, kt, for his service and one mark sterling in cash, of one acre of arable land in the vill of Ixworth Thorpe, whereof half an acre is in the field beyond *Banegrave* beside the land of William, abutting at one headland on the land of Thomas son of Cecily[a], and the other half an acre is in the field called *Northolm* beside the land of William son of Adam, abutting at one headland on the common pasture of Ixworth Thorpe, be there more or less, to hold and to have of the grantor and her heirs by William and his heirs or whosoever to whom he may wish to grant, sell or otherwise assign it, freely, quit, well, peaceably and by inheritance, rendering therefrom annually to the grantor and her heirs a clove at Easter for all services, aids, all manner of suit of court and demands. Warranty is granted against all persons in perpetuity. Sealed in witness.

Hiis testibus: Radulfo de Berdewell', Johanne filio Willelmi de eadem, Roberto ultra aquam, Roberto de Rekynghal', Waltero le Spenser, Radulfo filio Symonis de Thorp', Willelmo filio Ade de eadem, Roberto le Syre, Willelmo le Syre, Johanne le Syre, et aliis.

Ixworth Thorpe, Monday 11 Jan. 1283

a presumably Cecily of Brakelond.

12. Quitclaim by Alice widow of Ralph Cassamerre to William son of the said Ralph of all right and claim which she had or might have in one and a half acres of land in the field of Ixworth Thorpe lying between the lands of *dominus* William of Pakenham on both sides, of which one headland abuts on the embankment which is called *Thorpepond*, so that henceforth neither Alice nor anyone in her name may have any right or legal claim in the land, and for this quitclaim William gave 5s sterling. Sealed in witness.
Hiis testibus: Johanne filio Willelmi, Roberto ultra aquam, Willelmo de Wilyngham, Roberto le Syre, Radulfo filio Symonis, Petro de Thorp', et aliis.

Ixworth Thorpe, 15 June 1281

13. Quitclaim by Alice daughter of Geoffrey Hubert of Ixworth Thorpe for herself and her heirs to *dominus* William of Pakenham, his heirs or assigns, of all her right and claim which she had or might have in all the land situated in the field called *Northernedych* with all its appurtenances without reservation, so that henceforth neither Alice nor her heirs may have any right or legal claim in the said land with its appurtenances. Sealed in [*fo. 3v*] witness.
Hiis testibus: Willelmo de Thelnitham, Radulfo de Berdewell', Ricardo de Suthenton, Roberto ultra aquam, Roberto de Rekynghal', Waltero le Spenser, Roberto de Blakebergh, Radulfo filio Symonis, Willelmo filio Ade, Ricardo de Bernham, Roberto le Syre, Petro de Thorp', et aliis.

[Third quarter of thirteenth century, before 1283]

14. Grant in heredity by Alice daughter of Geoffrey Hubert of Ixworth Thorpe to *dominus* William of Pakenham, kt, for his service and 10s sterling in cash, of one acre of arable land in the field of Ixworth Thorpe beside the land of William, abutting at one headland on *Bromsclyde*, be there more or less, to hold and to have of the grantor and her heirs by William and his heirs or whosoever to whom he may wish to grant, sell or to otherwise assign it, freely, quit, well, peaceably and by inheritance, rendering therefrom annually to the grantor and her heirs a clove at Easter for all services, aids, all manner of suit of court and demands. Warranty is granted against all persons in perpetuity. Sealed in witness.
Hiis testibus: Johanne filio Willelmi, Roberto ultra aquam, Waltero le Spenser, Roberto de Rekynhal', Roberto de Drenkyston, Radulfo filio Symonis, Ricardo de Berningham, Galfrido Louwyn, Roberto le Syre, Hubert de Angrihal', et aliis.

Ixworth Thorpe, 9 July 1282

15. Grant in heredity by Alice daughter of Geoffrey Hubert of Ixworth Thorpe to *dominus* William of Pakenham, for his service and for 40s sterling which he gave to her in cash, of one and a half acres of arable land in the field of Ixworth Thorpe beside the land of John Hereward, abutting at one headland on the land of William and at the other on that of Simon of Gislingham (*Gesselingham*), be there more or less, to hold and to have of the grantor and her heirs by William and his heirs or whosoever to whom he may wish to grant, sell or otherwise assign it, freely, quit, well, peaceably and by inheritance, rendering therefrom annually to the grantor and her heirs a clove at Easter for all services, aids and secular demands. Warranty is granted against all persons in perpetuity. Sealed in witness.
Hiis testibus: Willelmo de Thelnitham, Radulfo de Berdewell', Roberto ultra aquam, Roberto de Rekynghal', Waltero le Spenser, Roberto de Drenkyston', Radulfo filio Symonis, Willelmo filio Ade, Ricardo de Bernham, Roberto le Syre, Willelmo le Syre, Petro de Thorp', et aliis.

[Late thirteenth century, before 1290]

16. Grant in heredity by William son of Adam of Ixworth Thorpe to William of Pakenham, kt, for his service and 20s of silver in cash, of two and a half acres of arable land in the field of the foresaid vill lying between the lands of William on both sides, abutting at one headland on *Dedemor*, and all that part which pertains to the grantor in the wood called *Wlfothieshg*, to hold and to have of the grantor and his heirs by William, his heirs, and assigns, freely, quit, well, peaceably and by inheritance, rendering therefrom annually to the grantor and his heirs a clove at the feast of Edward the Confessor [5 Jan.], for all services, aids and secular demands. Warranty is granted against all persons in perpetuity. Sealed in witness.
Hiis testibus: [*fo. 4r*] Willelmo Fromund, Radulfo Symund, Johanne le Syre, Johanne de Londismere, Roberto de Blakebergh, Galfrido filio Louwyn, Symone de Walsham, Petro de Thorp', et aliis.

[Late thirteenth century, before 1290]

17. Grant in heredity by William le Warde of Ixworth Thorpe to *dominus* William of Pakenham, kt, for 20s sterling in cash, of the whole pasture which he had in Ixworth Thorpe as it lies in the parcel next to the herbage of *dominus* William, to have and to hold by *dominus* William, his heirs, and assigns, freely, quit, well, peaceably, in fee and heredity. Warranty is granted against all persons in perpetuity. Sealed in witness.
Hiis testibus: Radulfo de Berdewell', Johanne filio Willelmi, Roberto ultra aquam, Symone de Gesselingham, Roberto de Blakebergh, Johanne Louwin, Johanne le Syre, Thoma Revel, Henrico le talyur, Alixandro de Stanton', Roberto le Syre, Petro de Thorp', et aliis.

[Late thirteenth century, before 1290]

18. Quitclaim by Adam son of Simon of Ixworth Thorpe for himself and his heirs to William of Pakenham, of all his right and claim which he had or in anyway might have in his share pertaining to the wood which is called

Mundevillesheg near the wood of William son of Robert of Bardwell (*Berdewell'*), for 15s of silver in cash, to have and to hold by him, his heirs and assigns without objection or claim by Adam's heirs in perpetuity, freely, quit and by inheritance. Sealed in witness.
Hiis testibus: Galfrido de Thorp', Radulfo filio Symonis, Willelmo le Syre, Roberto le Syre, Johanne le Syre, Galfrido Hubert de Thorp, Willelmo filio Roberti de Berdewell, Eadmundo Tolle, Adam de Suthenton', Roberto ultra aquam, Waltero de Herdford,[a] Semano de Wilyngham, Johanne Scot, et aliis.

[Mid-thirteenth century, before 1263]

The original charter exists as BL Harleian Charter 56 I 22, 150mm wide x 60mm; seal, round, approx. 30mm, natural wax, eight-pointed star; SIGIL ADE DE TORP.

a Hertford.

19. Grant in heredity by William le Warde of Ixworth Thorpe to *dominus* William of Pakenham, kt, for nine marks of silver in cash, of five and a half acres of arable land in Ixworth Thorpe with the whole pasture that abuts on that land towards the south, lying between the lands of *dominus* William called *le Wong* on both sides of the meadow and at one headland on Broadwater (*Bradewater*) held of *dominus* William, be there more or less, to have and to hold by *dominus* William and his heirs or assigns, freely, quit, well, peaceably and by inheritance. Warranty is granted against all persons in perpetuity. Sealed in witness.
Hiis testibus: Radulfo de Berdewell', Johanne filio Willelmi de eadem, Roberto ultra aquam de eadem, Symone de Geselingham, Roberto de Brakebergh, Ricardo de Bernham, Johanne Lowyn, Roberto le Syre, Johanne le Syre, Thoma Revel, Henrico le talyur, Alixandro de Stanton', et aliis.

[Late thirteenth century, before 1290]

A fragment of this charter survives as BL Harleian Charter 57 E 10, original size approx. 175mm wide x 100mm; seal, round, approx. 30mm, natural wax, animal design, possibly a running horse, illegible.

20. Grant in heredity by William le Warde of Ixworth Thorpe to *dominus* William of Pakenham, kt, of one piece of land in Ixworth Thorpe called *Sparwestoft* lying between the land of *dominus* William on the one side and that of Simon of Gislingham (*Gesselingham*) on the other, be there more or less, to have and to hold by *dominus* William and his heirs or his assigns, freely, quit, well, peaceably, [*fo. 4v*] in fee and by perpetual inheritance. Warranty is granted against all persons in perpetuity, and for this grant, gift and warranty *dominus* William gave 25s of silver in cash. Sealed in witness.
Hiis testibus: Radulfo de Berdewell', Symone de Geselingham, Roberto ultra aquam, Roberto de Drenkyston', Roberto de Blakebergh, Johanne le Syre, Petro de Thorp', Thoma Revel, Henrico le talyur, Alixandro de Stanton', Roberto filio Radulfi, Johanne Louwin, et aliis.

[Late thirteenth century, before 1290]

21. Grant in heredity by William le Warde of Ixworth Thorpe to *dominus* William of Pakenham, kt, for his service and one mark of silver in cash, of three roods of arable land and five roods of meadow in the vill of Ixworth Thorpe, of which the said three roods of land lie in the field called *Wilgemare* between the lands of *dominus* William on both sides, abutting at one headland on the common pasture of Ixworth Thorpe, and the said five roods of meadow lie in *Dedemor* beside the meadow of William, abutting at one headland on the fishery of *dominus* William, be there more or less, to hold and to have of the grantor and his heirs by *dominus* William and his heirs or whosoever to whom he may wish to grant, sell or otherwise assign them, freely, quit, well, peaceably and by inheritance, rendering therefrom annually to the grantor and his heirs a clove at Easter for all aids, all manner of suit of court and secular demands. Warranty is granted against all persons in perpetuity. Sealed in witness.
Hiis testibus: Willelmo de Thelnitham, Radulfo de Berdewell', Roberto ultra aquam, Roberto de Blakebergh, Radulfo filio Symonis, Willelmo de Wilyngham, Roberto de Bernigham, Roberto le Syre, Willelmo le Syre, Johanne le Syre, Alixandro de Stanton', Petro de Thorp', et aliis.

[Late thirteenth century, before 1290]

22. Grant in heredity by Robert of Drinkstone (*Drenkyston*) to *dominus* William of Pakenham, kt, of two acres of arable land in Ixworth Thorpe lying in the field called *Wodecroft* between the lands of Thomas, son of *dominus* William, on both sides, abutting at one headland on the road called *Northerndych*. The foresaid Robert, in order that this grant, gift, ratification, and confirmation may be held by the grantee, acknowledges by this document the right of Thomas in this land, be there more or less, to have and to hold by Thomas, his heirs, and assigns of the capital lord of the fee by the due and customary service, freely, well, peaceably and in heredity for all services, customs, charges and demands. Warranty is granted against all persons in perpetuity, and for this grant, gift, and acknowledgement Thomas gave to the grantor two marks of silver in cash. Sealed in witness.
Hiis testibus; Roberto Barnard, Alberico de Wykes, Petro de Thelnitham, Johanne de Berdewell', Eadmundo le Spenser, Roberto le Blakebergh, Waltero Kenne, Roberto filio Radulfi, Willelmo le Warde, Johanne le Syre, Petro de Thorp', Alixandro de Stanton', et multis aliis.

[1290 x 1305]

23. Grant in heredity by Robert of Drinkstone (*Drenkyston*) [*fo. 5r*] to Thomas son of *dominus* William of Pakenham, kt, for twenty marks sterling in cash, of two messuages, twenty acres of land, and three acres of meadow with appurtenances in Bardwell (*Berdewell*) and Ixworth Thorpe, to have and to hold of the capital lords of the fees by Thomas, his heirs, and assigns, freely, quit, well, peaceably and by inheritance, by the due and customary service. Warranty is granted against all persons in perpetuity. Sealed in witness.
Hiis testibus: Johanne filio Willelmi de Berdewell', Ricardo filio Henrici de Sancto Eadmundo, Alberico de Wykes, Henrico de Berdewell', Johanne de

Suthenton', Eadmundo le Spenser, Johanne de Buxal', Willelmo le Butcou', Waltero Kenne, Petro de Thorp', Willelmo Warde, Willelmo Anlwy.

Bardwell, 22 April 1305

23a. Final concord made in the *curia regis* at Cattishall (*Catteshill*) on 23 February 1276 ('die dominica proxima post festum beati Petri in cathedra anno regni regis Edwardi filii Regis Henrici quarto') before Thomas of Welland and John of Mettingham, justices itinerant, and later recorded in the same *curia regis* at Westminster on 3 May 1276 ('a die pasche in unum mensem anno eodem') before Roger of Seaton, Mr Richard of Staines, John of Cobham, Mr Ralph of Farningham, Thomas of Welland and John de Luvetot, justices, between Lawrence son of Fulk of Pakenham and Amicia his wife, Alured of Drinkstone (*Drencheston*) and Cecilia his wife, plaintiffs, and William of Pakenham, defendant, relating to one messuage, one carucate of land and ten acres of meadow with appurtenances in Ixworth Thorpe, whereof an assize of *mort d'ancestor* was held between them in the same *curia* and it was resolved thus: that Lawrence, Amicia, Alured and Cecilia acknowledged that the tenement with its appurtenances was William's as of right, and they acknowledged, remitted and quitclaimed this to William and his heirs for themselves and the heirs of Amicia and Cecilia in perpetuity in return for a payment by William of 80 marks of silver.

PRO, CP 25/1/215/33 no. 5; approx. 270 x 70mm.

23b. Final concord made in the *curia regis* at Westminster on 6 October 1305 before Ralph de Hengham, William de Bereford, Elias of Beckingham, Peter Mallore, William Howard and Lambert of Threekingham, justices, between Thomas son of William of Pakenham, plaintiff, and Robert of Drinkstone (*Drencheston*), defendant, relating to a plea for two messuages, twenty acres of land and three acres of meadow with appurtenances in Bardwell (*Berdewell*) and Ixworth Thorpe, whereby Robert acknowledged that the tenements with appurtenances were Thomas's as of right given him by Robert. And for this acknowledgement and final concord Thomas conceded to Robert the tenements with appurtenances to have and to hold by Robert of Thomas and his heirs for the whole of Robert's life, rendering therefrom one rose on the feast of the Nativity of St John the Baptist [24 June] for all services, customs, and exactions that pertain thereto, and to the capital lords of the fee all other services that pertain to the tenements. And after Robert's death, the tenements are to revert wholly to Thomas and his heirs quit of Robert's heirs, to have and to hold of the capital lords of the fee in perpetuity.

PRO, CP 25/1/216/46 no. 28; approx. 262 x 148mm.

24. Grant in heredity by Alice Dost of Ixworth Thorpe to Robert of Drinkstone (*Drenkyston*) of Bardwell (*Berdewell*), for his service and for ten marks of silver in cash as entry fine, of a messuage with all appurtenances pertaining to it and

with everything growing on it and revenues from it with all services, rights of pasture and grazing, and all other easements (*asyamentis*), to have and to hold of the capital lords of the fees by Robert and his heirs or his assigns or whosoever to whom he may wish to grant, sell or otherwise assign them, freely, quit, well and in peace, in fee and heredity, rendering therefrom annually to the capital lords of the fees the due and customary service, and to the grantor and her heirs for warranty a clove at the feast of Edward the Confessor [5 Jan.], for all services, aids, customs, suit of court and all secular demands. Warranty is granted against all persons in perpetuity. Sealed in witness.
Hiis testibus: Symone de Geselingham, Waltero Kenne, Roberto le Syre, Radulfo de Bardewell', Johanne filio Willelmi, Roberto ultra aquam, Eadmundo le Spenser, Johanne fratre suo, et aliis.

Ixworth Thorpe, Tuesday 15 Dec. 1293

25. Grant in heredity by Simon son of Alan of Gislingham (*Gesselingham*) to Richard son of Matilda le Ros of Sapiston, for his homage and service and for ten marks of silver in cash, of five acres of arable land lying in the field of Honington (*Hunegeton'*), of which the tithe of the meadow is due to the church of Sapiston (*Sapeston'*), of which one piece lies in the quarter (*quarentena*) which is called *Passewong* between the land of David son of Nicholas on the one side and the land of Thomas son of Bartholomew on the other, of which one headland abuts on the common pasture of Honington, and one piece lies in the same field between the land of the church of Honington and that of William of Pakenham, of which one headland abuts on the herbage [*fo. 5v*] of John le Man of Honington, and one piece lies in the same field beside the land of Geoffrey son of Nicholas of Honington, of which one headland abuts on the road that leads from Sapiston to Troston (*Stroston'*), be there more or less, to have and to hold of the grantor and his heirs by Richard and his heirs or his assigns and whosoever to whom he may wish to grant, sell, bequeath, or assign it, freely, quit, well, peaceably, in fee and heredity, rendering therefrom annually to the grantor and his heirs or his assigns 12d at two annual terms, that is, at Michaelmas 6d and at Easter 6d, for all services, aids, customs, suit of court and hundred, and all other secular demands, save service to the lord king when it occurs, namely, towards a scutage (*ad scutagium*) of 20s, ½d, and for more, more, and for less, less. Warranty is granted against all persons in perpetuity. Sealed in witness.
Hiis testibus: domino Rogero de Walsham, milite, domino Eustachio de Berningham, milite, Berardo de Watysfeld, Willelmo de Thelnitham, Radulfo de Berdewell', Johanne filio Willelmi, Roberto ultra aquam, Roberto de Blakeberth', Radulfo filio Symonis de Thorp', Radulfo filio Radulfi, Ricardo de Bernham, et aliis.

[Third quarter of thirteenth century, before 1283]

25a. Agreement between *dominus* William of Pakenham, kt, on the one hand and Richard le Ros of Ixworth Thorpe on the other, whereby Richard conceded and demised at farm to William, for 60s of silver which Richard gave in cash, five acres of land with appurtenances in the fields of Honington (*Hunegheton'*), of

which two acres lie in the field called *Passewong* beside the land of Geoffrey le Minyt, and two acres lie in the same field beside the land formerly of David the smith (*faber*), and one acre lies in the same field beside the land of the church of Honington (*Hunegheton'*), be there more or less, to have and to hold by William, his heirs or assigns from Michaelmas 1287 for the full twelve years following, and Richard and his heirs or assigns shall acquit and defend the land for William, his heirs or assigns from every form of service and custom against any person. And at the end of the term, the whole of the land shall revert fully to Richard, his heirs or assigns or whosoever after the death of Richard has a right in the land, without objection by William, his heirs or assigns. And if it should happen that Richard, or whoever has a right in the land after the death of Richard, is willing, and the foresaid 60s is repaid before the end of the term to William, his heirs or assigns, the whole of that land, saving to William, his heirs or assigns his crops growing there at that time, shall fully revert to him without objection of William, his heirs or assigns. Sealed in witness in the form of a chirograph to which each has affixed his seal.
Hiis testibus: Willelmo de Thelnitham, Radulfo de Berdewell', Ricardo de Suthenton', Roberto ultra aquam, Roberto de Brakeberghe, Willelmo de Wylingham, Ricardo de Bernham, Thoma Revel, Henrico le tayllur, Alexandro de Stanton', Petro de Thorp', et aliis.

[Third quarter of thirteenth century, before 1283]

Harleian Charter 54 E 57. Single-sheet original, bottom portion of a chirograph, 218mm wide x 102mm; seal, round, approx. 25mm, green wax, illegible.

26. Notification by Simon of Gislingham (*Gesselyngham*) and Matilda his wife that they and their heirs and assigns are obliged to *dominus* William of Pakenham, kt, and his heirs or assigns, for 20d of silver in annual rent for a messuage which they bought from William in the vill of Ixworth Thorpe which the same William acquired from the prioress and held as a tenant of Bungay (*Bunegeye*) in return for a payment to the prioress of 30d annually, that is at Michaelmas 15d and at Easter 15d. And if it should happen that Simon, his heirs or assigns default and do not pay the 30d at the aforesaid terms, then William, his heirs or assigns may distrain on Simon, his heirs or assigns in all the aforesaid lands and tenements in the vill of Ixworth Thorpe until full satisfaction shall have been made to William, his heirs or assigns for the rent of 30d, just as contained in the charter of enfeoffment which William gave to Simon and is in this notification, so that the agreement might endure in perpetuity. Sealed in witness.

Ixworth Thorpe, Wednesday 24 Nov. 1294

27. Grant in heredity by Simon son of Alan of Gislingham (*Gesselingham*) to *dominus* William of Pakenham, for his service and 16s sterling in cash, of one acre of arable land lying in the field of Ixworth Thorpe at Longfurlong (*Longeforlong*) between the land of Robert Dispenser (*le Spenser*) on the one side and that of Botild de Angirhal on the other, of which one headland abuts towards the north on the land of William, to have and to hold of the grantor and his heirs

by William, his heirs or assigns or whosoever to whom he may wish to grant, sell or otherwise assign it, freely, quit, well, peaceably and by inheritance, rendering therefrom annually to the grantor and his heirs 2d at Michaelmas for all services, customs, suits of court, aids and demands. Warranty is granted [*fo. 6r*] against all persons in perpetuity. Sealed in witness.
Hiis testibus: dominis Willelmo de Creketot, Reginaldo Pecche, militibus, Radulfo de Berdewell, Johanne filio Willelmi de eadem, Radulfo filio Symonis de Thorp', Ricardo de Bernham de eadem, Petro de Thorp', Willelmo le Warde, Roberto le Syre, Willelmo le Syre, Roberto de Drenkyston', Roberto de Blakebergh, et aliis.

[Late thirteenth century, before 1290]

28. Grant in heredity by Simon of Gislingham (*Gesselingham*) to *dominus* William of Pakenham, kt, for his service and 100s sterling which he gave as entry fine, of five acres of land in Honington (*Hunegeton'*), of which one piece lies in the field called *Passewong* between the land of John son of David on the one part and that of Thomas son of Bartholomew on the other, and one piece lies in the same field between the land of the church of Honington and that of Alice Croil, and one piece lies in the same field beside the land of Geoffrey son of Nicholas, be there more or less, to have and to hold by William, his heirs or assigns, of the grantor and his heirs or whosoever to whom he may wish to grant, sell or otherwise assign them, freely, quit, well, peaceably and by inheritance, rendering therefrom to the grantor and his heirs a clove at Easter, and to the two capital lords 12d of silver at Michaelmas and at Easter for all services, customs, all manner of suit of court, aids and demands. Warranty is granted against all persons in perpetuity. Sealed in witness.
Hiis testibus: Radulfo de Berdewell, Johanne filio Willelmi, Ricardo de Suthenton', Roberto ultra aquam, Petro de Thorp', Thoma Ryvel, Alixandro de Stanton', Ricardo de Bernham, Roberto le Syre, Willelmo le Warde, Roberto Greund, Henrico le talyur de Ixeworth', et aliis.

[Third quarter of thirteenth century, before 1283]

29. Quitclaim by Richard son of Matilda le Ros of Sapiston, on behalf of himself and his heirs, to Simon son of Alan of Gislingham and his heirs or assigns of all right which he has and claim which he had or might have or in anyway henceforth may have in five acres of land in the field of Honington (*Hunegeton'*) with all its appurtenances, which he once bought from Simon and held from him for 12d a year, so that neither *dominus* Richard, his heirs nor his assigns may henceforth have any right or claim in the said land with its appurtenances. Sealed in witness.
Hiis testibus: Willelmo de Thelnitham, Radulfo Symund, Ricardo de Bernham, Willelmo le Warde, Roberto Grehund, Alano Canne, Roberto le Syre, Johanne le Syre, Petro de Thorp', Alixandro de Stanton', Henrico le talyur, et aliis.

[Third quarter of thirteenth century, before 1283]

30. Grant in heredity by William son of Nicholas le Ros of Ixworth Thorpe to Simon of Gislingham (*Geslingham*), for his homage and service and one mark of silver which he gave as entry fine, of one acre of arable land in the field of Ixworth Thorpe which is called Longfurlong (*Longeforlong*) between the land of Robert Dispenser (*le Spenser*) and that of Botild de Angirhal, abutting at one headland on the road which is called *Wallegateweye* and the other on the land of *dominus* William of Pakenham, kt, be there more or less, to have and to hold of the grantor and his heirs by Simon, his heirs, [*fo. 6v*] and assigns or whosoever to whom he may wish to grant, sell, bequeath, or otherwise assign it, freely, quit, well and peaceably, in fee and by perpetual inheritance, rendering therefrom annually to the grantor and his heirs 2d at two annual terms, that is, at Michaelmas 1d and at Easter 1d, for all services, aids, customs, suits of court and all secular demands. Warranty is granted against all persons in perpetuity. Sealed in witness.
Hiis testibus: domino Willelmo de Pakynham, milite, domino Reginaldo Pecche de Stouwe, milite, Radulfo de Berdewell, Ricardo de Suthenton' de eadem, Radulfo filio Symonis de Thorp', Willelmo le Syre de eadem, Roberto le Syre, et aliis.

[Third quarter of thirteenth century, before 1283]

31. Grant in heredity by Simon of Gislingham (*Gyslingham*) to *dominus* William of Pakenham, kt, in exchange for a messuage formerly of the prioress and convent of Bungay (*Bunegeye*) which William gave to the grantor and Matilda his wife, of three roods of arable land in Ixworth Thorpe in the field beyond Broadwater (*Bradewater*) beside the land of William which he acquired from the prioress and convent of Bungay with the whole pasture pertaining to the foresaid three roods of land, be there more or less, to hold and to have by William and his heirs or assigns, freely, quit, well, peaceably, in fee and heredity. Warranty is granted. Sealed in witness.
Hiis testibus: Radulfo de Berdewell, Johanne filio Willelmi, Willelmo de Thelnitham, Petro filio suo, Roberto de Blakebergh, Willelmo le Warde, Johanne Louwyne, Roberto le Syre, Alixandro sutore, Thoma Revel, Henrico le talyur, Petro de Thorp', et aliis.

[Late thirteenth century, before 1290]

32. Grant in heredity by Simon of Gislingham (*Geslingham*) to *dominus* William of Pakenham, for his service and 40s sterling in cash, of two acres of arable land and one and a half roods of meadow in the vill of Ixworth Thorpe, of which one acre of land lies in the field called *Northolm* between the land of the grantor and the common pasture, abutting at one headland on the land of Walter Kenne, and three roods lie in the same field beside the land formerly of Paulyn Feloun, abutting at one headland on the common pasture, and one rood in the same field beside the land of Walter Kenne, abutting at one headland on the land of the said William, and the said meadow lies in *Dedemor* beside the meadow of William, abutting at one headland on the common road, be there more or less, to hold and to have of the grantor and his heirs by William, his heirs, or assigns, freely, quit,

well, peaceably and by inheritance, rendering to the capital lords of the fee due and customary service and to the grantor and his heirs a clove at Easter for all services, customs, aids and secular demands. Warranty is granted against all persons in perpetuity. Sealed in witness.
Hiis testibus: Johanne filio Willelmi, Roberto ultra aquam, Waltero le Spenser, Roberto de Brakebregh, Radulfo Symund, Willelmo filio Davidi, Ricardo de Suthenton', Nicholao Robyn, Petro de Thorp', et aliis.

[Third quarter thirteenth century, before 1282]

33. [*fo. 7r*] Grant in heredity by Simon of Gislingham (*Geslingham*) to *dominus* William of Pakenham, kt, for his service and 20s sterling in cash, of two acres of arable land in the vill of Ixworth Thorpe in the field called *Northolm*, of which half an acre lies beside the land of Alice Binchard, abutting at one headland on the common pasture, and half an acre lies beside the land of Walter son of Adam of Thorpe (*Thorp'*), abutting at one headland on the foresaid common, and half an acre of land lies beside that of William of Pakenham, abutting at one headland on the foresaid common, and one acre lies beside the land of William of Willingham (*Wilyngham*),[a] abutting at one headland on the said common, be there more or less, to hold and to have of the grantor and his heirs by William and his heirs or whosoever to whom he may wish to grant, sell or otherwise assign it, freely, quit, well, peaceably and by inheritance, rendering therefrom annually to the grantor and his heirs a clove at Easter for all services, aids, all manner of suit of court and secular demands. Warranty is granted against all persons in perpetuity. Sealed in witness.
Hiis testibus: Johanne filio Willelmi de Berdewell', Radulfo de Berdewell', Roberto ultra aquam, Ricardo de Suthenton', Radulfo filio Symonis, Willelmo filio Ade, Willelmo de Wilyngham, Roberto le Syre, Huberto de Ayngirhal', et aliis.

Ixworth Thorpe, Tuesday 10 Nov. 1282

a This adds up to 2½ acres.

34. Grant in heredity by Simon of Gislingham (*Geselyngham*) to *dominus* William of Pakenham, kt, for his service and 40s sterling in cash, of one cottage (*cotagium*) and three roods of land with buildings in the vill of Ixworth Thorpe beside the messuage and croft of John Hereward, abutting at one headland on the common of Ixworth Thorpe; he furthermore grants to William a quarter of the meadow in *Dedemor* with the heath situated beside the meadow of John le Syre, be there more or less, to hold and to have of the grantor and his heirs by William and his heirs or whosoever to whom he may wish to grant, sell or otherwise assign it, freely, quit, well, peaceably and by inheritance, rendering therefrom annually to the grantor and his heirs a clove at Easter for all services, aids, all manner of suit of court and secular demands. Warranty is granted against all persons in perpetuity. Sealed in witness.
Hiis testibus: Willelmo de Thelnitham, Radulfo de Berdewell, Johanne filio

Willelmi, Roberto ultra aquam, Roberto de Rekynghal', Roberto de Blakebergh, Radulfo filio Symonis, Willelmo le Syre, Johanne le Syre, et aliis.

[Late thirteenth century, before 1290]

35. Grant in heredity by Simon son of Alan of Gislingham (*Geslyngham*) to *dominus* William of Pakenham, kt, for his service and 20s sterling in cash, of one acre and half a rood of arable land, of which half an acre lies in the vill of Ixworth Thorpe in the field called *Schamelocis* beside the land of William, and half an acre lies in the same field [*fo. 7v*] between the land of William on the one side and that of William of Willingham (*Wilyngham*) on the other, and half an acre[a] lies in the vill of Honington (*Hunegeton'*) in the field of *Blodhowe* beside the land of William le Warde, be there more or less, to have and to hold of the grantor and his heirs by William and his heirs or whosoever to whom he may wish to grant, sell or assign it, freely, quit, well, peaceably and by inheritance, rendering therefrom annually to the grantor and his heirs a clove at Easter for all services, aids, all manner of suit of court and demands. Warranty is granted against all persons in perpetuity. Sealed in witness.

Hiis testibus: Willelmo de Thelnitham, Radulfo de Berdewell', Johanne filio Willelmi, Roberto ultra aquam, Roberto de Blakebergh, Radulfo filio Symonis, Ricardo de Bernham, Willelmo filio Ade, Willelmo le Syre, Roberto le Syre, Johanne le Syre, Petro de Thorp', et aliis.

[Late thirteenth century, before 1290]

a This adds up to 1½ acres. There is no mention of the rood of land.

36. Quitclaim by Simon of Gislingham (*Gesslyngham*) for himself and his heirs to *dominus* William of Pakenham and his heirs or assigns, for 2s of silver in cash, of 2d in annual rents which he held from one acre of land in the vill of Ixworth Thorpe in the field called Longfurlong (*Longeferlong*) which was acquired from the grantor, to hold and to have by William and his heirs or assigns, freely, quit, well, peaceably and by inheritance, so that neither Simon nor his heirs nor anyone in his name may henceforth demand any right or have any claim in the said rents. Sealed so that the terms of the charter may endure in perpetuity.

Hiis testibus: Willelmo de Thelnitham, Johanne de Berdewell, Roberto ultra aquam, Ricardo de Suthenton', Roberto de Blakebergh, Nicholao Robyn, Ricardo de Bernham, Petro de Thorp', et aliis.

[Third quarter of thirteenth century, before 1283]

37. Grant in heredity by Geoffrey son of Walter of Thorpe (*Thorp'*) to William of Pakenham, for five marks of silver in cash, of his messuage with all buildings and all the land and tenement which he had in the vill of Ixworth Thorpe with all its liberties and appurtenances without any reservation, to have and to hold by William and his heirs or his assigns, rendering therefrom to the lord of the fee 6d at two annual terms, that is, at Michaelmas 3d and at Easter 3d, for all services,

customs, suit of court and all exactions and demands. Warranty is granted against all persons in perpetuity. Sealed in witness.
Hiis testibus: domino Roberto de Wykes, Thoma de Stanton', Johanne de Stanton', Henrico de Berdewell, Willelmo filio Roberti, Galfrido de Thorp', Roberto de Berneys, Johanne de Pakynham, Waltero de Herford, Johanne de Horthach, Briano mariscallo, Willelmo de Ponte, Adam de Wallepol et aliis.

[Mid thirteenth century, before 1263]

38. Quitclaim by John son of Geoffrey of Thorpe (*Thorp*') for himself and his heirs in perpetuity to Geoffrey, Thomas, Beatrice and Agnes, children of the said Geoffrey his father, of all right which he has and claim which he had or in anyway might have in all his land in the vill of Ixworth Thorpe which Geoffrey, his father, freely and voluntarily conceded and gave to Geoffrey, Thomas, Agnes, and Beatrice, to have and to hold by them [*fo. 8r*] and their heirs or assigns without any reservation to John or his heirs, and for this gift, concession, and quitclaim they gave 20s sterling in cash. Sealed in witness.
Hiis testibus: Willelmo filio Roberti de Berdewell, Roberto ultra aquam, Adam de Suthenton', Radulfo filio Symonis de Thorp', Willelmo le Syre de eadem, Willelmo Louwyn, Johanne de Lyvermere, Jacobo clerico, et aliis.

[Third quarter of thirteenth century, before 1280]

39. Quitclaim by Margaret widow of Geoffrey of Thorpe (*Thorp'*) to William of Pakenham and his heirs or assigns for half a mark of silver in cash, of 16d in annual rents which each year she received from William for the tenement which Galiena widow of Simon Goddyld held in Ixworth Thorpe, without any reservation, to hold and to have by William and his heirs or his assigns, without claim by her or by any one on her behalf in perpetuity. So that Margaret cannot go against this concession, remission, and quitclaim, this deed has been issued and sealed.
Hiis testibus: domino Matheo de Thelnitham, Willelmo patre meo (*sic*, for suo?), Johanne de Pakynham, Roberto ultra aquam de Berdewell', Radulfo le Meyster de Ixeworth', Thoma fratre suo, Roberto de Drenkyston', Petro de Thorp', et aliis.

[Late thirteenth century, before 1300]

40. Grant in heredity by Geoffrey son of William of Thorpe (*Thorp'*) to Ralph Leun son of Walter of the same place, for his homage and service and for 10s of silver in cash, of two acres of arable land in the field of Ixworth Thorpe lying in the field which is called *Scamelocys* between the land of Simon son of William and that of Alice Vidrie of Ixworth Thorpe, be there more or less, to have and to hold of the grantor and his heirs, freely, quit and honourably by Ralph and his heirs or assigns or whosoever to whom he may wish to assign it, by the service of 2d of silver rendered annually to the grantor and his heirs, namely, at Michaelmas 1d and at Easter 1d, for all services, customs, aids, and exactions, save service of the lord king, namely, towards a scutage of 20s, 2d, and for more, more, and for

less, less. Warranty is granted against all persons in perpetuity. Sealed so that the terms of this charter may endure as valid.
Hiis testibus: Willelmo de Thorp', Roberto filio Normanni, Willelmo Breton', Rogero de Boxstede, Symone Petro Syre (*sic*), Willelmo Syre, Galfrido Hubert, et multis aliis.

[Mid thirteenth century, before 1263]

41. Grant in heredity by William son of Geoffrey of Thorpe to John son of Miles de Verdun, his heirs and assigns, of a croft with its land in the vill of Ixworth Thorpe, just as enclosed by hedges and ditches, lying between the land of the prior of Ixworth on the one side and that of Nicholas Schanke on the other, with one headland extending to the stream (*aquam pluvientem*) called *Becke* and the other headland on the king's highway to the east, to have and to hold by John and his heirs or assigns and by their heirs of the grantor and his heirs freely, quit, wholly, by inheritance, well and in peace in perpetuity, rendering therefrom annually to the grantor and his heirs 1d at Michaelmas for all services, aids, exactions, suit of court and secular demands, saving as much royal service as pertains to the land of the same fee in the same vill. Warranty is granted against all persons in perpetuity. And for this grant John gave the grantor 30s as entry fine. [*fo. 8v*] The grantor has appended his seal.
Hiis testibus: dominis Matheo de Thelnitham, Ricardo de Wykes, Willelmo de Thelnitham, Galfrido marechal, Johanne filio Willelmi de Berdewell', Radulfo de Berdewell', Roberto Ongelewe, Willelmo le Syre, Radulfo filio presbiteri, Willelmo patre rectore de Troston, Willelmo Louwyne, Radulfo clerico, et aliis.

Tuesday 25 April 1251, 26 April 1261 or 28 April 1271

The dating clause has 'anno regni Regis Henrici filii Regis Johannis quinto', but since the document will not allow a date that early, it seems likely that the scribe has omitted part of the regnal year.

42. Grant in heredity by Geoffrey of Thorpe (*Thorp'*) to William of Pakenham of a piece of land which is called *le Breche* with all its liberties and appurtenances lying between the land of William le Syre and Nicholas le Bor, be there more or less, and of two and a half acres of marsh with all its liberties and appurtenances in the vill of Ixworth Thorpe lying between his marsh and that of Henry Stegre, be there more or less, to have and to hold of the grantor and his heirs by the grantee and his heirs or whosoever to whom he may wish to grant, sell, bequeath or assign them or whithersoever he may give them, freely, quit, peaceably, in fee and by inheritance, rendering therefrom annually to the grantor and his heirs 3d at Michaelmas for all service, custom, exaction and demand. Warranty is granted against all, whether Jews or Christians. Sealed in witness.
Hiis testibus: domino Roberto de Wykes, milite, Radulfo de Berdewell', Henrico fratre suo, Thoma de Pakynham, Thoma de Stanton', Sayero de Stanton', Willelmo filio Roberti, Willelmo le Breton', Adam de Suthenton', Galfrido le Breton', Willelmo de Burch', et aliis.

[Mid thirteenth century, before 1263]

43. Demise by Geoffrey of Thorpe (*Thorp'*) to John of Pakenham, rector of the church of Hawkedon (*Haukedon'*), of all his fishery in the vill of Ixworth Thorpe with all its liberties and appurtenances, namely, from the mill that *dominus* William Blundys bought from the grantor as far as the fishery of Ixworth Priory near Sapiston, to have and to hold of the grantor and his heirs or his assigns by John and his assigns for the whole of his life as God grants it to him, rendering therefrom annually to the grantor and his heirs or assigns half a mark of silver at Easter for every custom, suit of court, secular service and demand. Warranty is granted against all for the whole of John's life, and after the death of Father John, the fishery with its appurtenances and liberties is to revert freely and quit to the grantor and his heirs without the objection of John's heirs or assigns. Sealed in witness.
Hiis testibus: Johanne de Pakynham, Willelmo fratre suo, Willelmo filio Roberti de Berdewell, Adam de Suthentoun, Roberto ultra aquam, Radulfo filio Symonis de Thorp', Willelmo le Syre de eadem, Thoma de Ixeworth, Waltero de Herdford, et aliis.

[Mid thirteenth century, before 1263]

43a. Agreement between William of Pakenham on the one hand and Geoffrey of Thorpe (*Thorp'*) on the other, whereby Geoffrey conceded and demised to William at farm, from 14 September 1256 for eight full years following, his whole fishery in the vill of Ixworth Thorpe with all its liberties and appurtenances, that is, from the mill which *dominus* William le Blund holds of Geoffrey as far as the fishery of the prior of Ixworth near Sapiston (*Sapeston'*); and the whole of his pasture which he had beside *Broding'* marsh, namely, by the marsh formerly of William *ultra aquam* as far as the pond of Richard son of Robert de Wykes, to have and to hold until the end of the term by William and his heirs or his assigns of Geoffrey and his heirs or assigns, freely, quit and peaceably, without secular demand. Warranty is granted against everyone. And for this concession and demise William gave Geoffrey 30s of silver. Written in the form of a chirograph and each has attached his seal.
Hiis testibus: Henrico de Berdewell', Edmundo fratre suo, Willelmo filio Roberti, Willelmo le Bretun, Galfrido fratre suo, Ada de Suthentone, Willelmo le Sire, et aliis.

[Mid thirteenth century, before Sept. 1256]

BL Harleian Charter 54 E 56. Single-sheet original in the form of a chirograph (lower portion), 176mm wide x 100mm, tag and seal missing.

44. Grant in heredity by Geoffrey son of William of Thorpe (*Thorp'*) to William of Pakenham, for his homage and service and for four marks of silver which he gave as entry fine, of five acres of land in the vill of Ixworth Thorpe with all its liberties and appurtenances without reservation, lying between the heath and land of Adam son of Simon of Thorpe (*Thorp'*), to have and to hold by William and his heirs or his assigns of the grantor and his heirs and assigns, freely, quit, peaceably, in fee and by inheritance, rendering therefrom annually to the grantor and

his heirs or his assigns 2d at Michaelmas for all service, custom, suit of court, exaction and demand. Warranty is granted against all by the grantor and his heirs in perpetuity. And he also grants 6d [*fo. 9r*] that he was accustomed to receive each year from William, that is, 4d from the land formerly of Hubert Hakun and 2d from the meadow that at some time Walkelin of Calne (*Calna*) held of the grantor. Sealed in witness.
Hiis testibus: Henrico de Berdewell', Eadmundo fratre suo, Willelmo filio Roberti, Willelmo le Breton', Adam de Suthenton', Roberto ultra aquam, Johanne de Stanton', Johanne de Pakynham, Willelmo fratre suo, Thoma de Pakynham, Willelmo le Syre, Waltero de Herforthd, et aliis.

[Mid thirteenth century, before 1263]

45. Grant in heredity by Thomas son of Geoffrey of Thorpe (*Thorp'*) to *dominus* William of Pakenham, kt, and Thomas and William his sons, for 24s sterling which they gave in cash, of one messuage and a croft in Ixworth Thorpe, just as they lie in length and width between the lands of *dominus* William on both sides, abutting at one headland on the common pasture of Ixworth Thorpe and the other on the road called *le Melleweye*, which they purchased from Geoffrey his brother from the fee that was formerly of Geoffrey of Thorpe (*Thorp'*), the grantor's father, to hold and to have by *dominus* William, Thomas, William and the heirs of the said Thomas and William, sons of *dominus* William, freely, quit, well, peaceably, in fee and heredity, rendering therefrom annually to the fraternity of St John the Baptist at the church of Ixworth Thorpe and to the fraternity of St John the Baptist of Battisford (*Batiford*) 2d for the souls of his ancestors, and if it should happen that Thomas and William fail to produce legitimate heirs of their bodies, then the messuage and croft with their appurtenances shall revert to the heirs of *dominus* William in perpetuity. Warranty is granted against all persons in perpetuity. Sealed in witness.
Hiis testibus: Willelmo de Thelnitham, Radulfo de Berdewell', Johanne filio Willelmi, Roberto ultra aquam, Symone de Gesslyngham, Roberto de Blakeberg', Roberto filio Radulfi, Galfrido fratre suo, Ricardo de Bernham, Henrico le talyur, et aliis.

[Late thirteenth century, before 1300]

46. Grant in heredity by John son of Geoffrey of Thorpe (*Thorp'*) to William of Necton (*Neketon'*), for two marks of silver in cash, of the homage and service of Gilbert le Bachelor (*Bachecheler*) of Ixworth Thorpe, that is, 4s of annual rents for a messuage and twelve acres of land with appurtenances in the vill of Ixworth Thorpe, namely, at Michaelmas 2s and at Easter 2s, with scutages, wardships, reliefs and escheats, to have and to hold of the grantor and his heirs by William of Necton and his heirs or his assigns, freely, quit, well, in fee and heredity, rendering therefrom annually to the grantor and his heirs a root of ginger (*radicem zenziberis*) at the feast of St Edmund [20 Nov.] for all services, suit of court, aids and exactions. Warranty is granted against all persons. Sealed so that the terms of this charter may endure in perpetuity.
Hiis testibus: domino Matheo de Thelnitham, Willelmo de Thelnitham, Salomon

de Ingham, Johanne marescallo de Troston', Galfrido Hubert de Thorp', Johanne de Geddyng, et aliis.

[Late thirteenth century, before 1290]

47. Grant in heredity by Walter son of Walter of Thorpe (*Thorp'*) to Alice his daughter, for her homage and service and for five marks of silver which she gave as entry fine, of a messuage with houses, trees, and buildings in the vill of Ixworth Thorpe [*fo. 9v*], and of all the land which falls to the grantor by right of inheritance, and of half an acre of land lying beside the said messuage in the toft formerly of William son of the late William of Thorpe, with all services, rights of pasture and grazing, and with all their appurtenances, without any reservation to the grantor and his heirs, or whosoever to whom she might wish to grant, sell, bequeath, or assign them or whithersoever she may give them, to have and to hold of the grantor and his heirs, freely, quit, well, in peace, in fee and heredity, rendering therefrom annually to the grantor and his heirs ½d at the feast of St Edmund [20 Nov.], and to the capital lords of the fee the due and customary service at the three statutory terms for all services, customs, exactions, aids, suit of court and demands. Warranty is granted against all men and women in perpetuity. Sealed in witness and security.
Hiis testibus: Willelmo de Thelnitham, Galfrido le marescal de Stroston', Radulfo filio Symonis de Thorp', Roberto ultra aquam de Berdewell, et multis aliis.

[Late thirteenth century, before 1290]

48. Grant in heredity by Geoffrey of Thorpe (*Thorp'*) to Mr Walkelin of Calne (*Calna*), rector of the church of Bardwell (*Berdewell'*), for his homage and service and for half a mark of silver which he gave as entry fine, of one acre of meadow lying in *Broddynge* between the meadow of the said Geoffrey and that of Robert *ultra aquam*, abutting at one headland on the river bank, to have and to hold of the grantor and his heirs by the grantee and his heirs or whosoever to whom he may wish to grant, sell or assign it, freely, quit, in fee, and heredity in perpetuity, rendering therefrom annually to the grantor and his heirs 1d at Easter for all services, aids, customs and exactions. Warranty is granted against all persons.
Hiis testibus: domino Roberto de Wykes, milite, domino Radulfo rectore ecclesie de Stanton', Thoma de Stanton', Johanne filio Willelmi, Henrico de Bek de Berdewell', Willelmo ultra aquam, et aliis.

[Mid thirteenth century, before 1263]

49. Grant in heredity by Geoffrey son of William of Thorpe (*Thorp'*) to Agnes his daughter, for her homage and service and for three marks of silver which she gave as entry fine, of three acres of arable land lying at *Stubyng*, abutting at one headland on the land of William of Bardwell (*Berdewell'*) and at the other on the land of the grantor; grant also to Agnes and her heirs of 4d-worth of land which William of Pakenham holds in the vill of Ixworth Thorpe from the land formerly of Hubert Hacun, to hold and to have the tenement of the grantor and his heirs by

Agnes and her heirs or whosoever to whom she may wish to grant, sell or assign it, freely, quit, well and in peace, in fee and heredity, rendering therefrom annually to the grantor and his heirs 1d at Easter, and to the scutage of the lord king when it occurs at 20s, 2d, and for more, more, and for less, less. Warranty is granted against all persons in perpetuity. Sealed in witness.
Hiis testibus: domino Matheo milite de Thelnitham, Henrico de Livermere, Johanne de eadem villa, Nicholao le Ros, Willelmo ad ecclesiam, Willelmo Page, et aliis.

[Mid thirteenth century, before 1263]

50. Grant in heredity by Geoffrey son of William of Thorpe to William of Pakenham, for four marks of silver which he gave as entry fine, of a piece of land lying in the vill of Ixworth Thorpe in the toft beside the marsh called *Brodyng*[a] beside *Brechelisbuk*, and of the whole pasture and marsh which he held beside the said land, and the use of the pond of *dominus* Richard de Wykes, and the whole of the marsh which he had between the marsh formerly of Geoffrey de Ambli and *Bro-* [*fo. 10r*] *chellisbusk* in the said marsh of *Brodyng* with all its liberties and appurtenances as freely and as fully as he held it, without any reservation, to have and to hold by William, his heirs and assigns of the grantor and his heirs, freely, quit, wholly, peaceably and in heredity, rendering therefrom annually to the grantor and his heirs at Michaelmas 2½d for all service, custom, exaction, suit of court and demand. Warranty is granted against all persons in perpetuity. Sealed in witness.
Hiis testibus: Henrico de Berdewell', Eadmundo fratre suo, Willelmo filio Roberti, Johanne de Stanton', Willelmo le Breton', Galfrido fratre suo, Johanne de Pakynham, Willelmo le Syre, Waltero de Herthford, Johanne le Frannes de Fuldon', et aliis.

[Mid thirteenth century, before 1263]

a Dedemor underlined for cancellation.

51. Quitclaim by William son of Geoffrey of Thorpe (*Thorp'*) for himself and his heirs or his assigns to *dominus* William of Pakenham, kt, and his heirs, for 100s sterling in cash, of all right which he has and claim which he had or in any way afterwards might have in all his lands and tenements which were formerly of Geoffrey his father in the vills of Ixworth Thorpe, Ixworth (*Ixeworth'*), and Bardwell (*Berdewell'*) without any reservation, as in messuages, arable lands, woods, meadows, rights of pasture and grazing, waters, roads, fish-ponds, fisheries, pastures, footpaths, homages, villeinages, and reliefs, wardships, escheats, along with the homages and rents of John de Hermstede, and also of all right which he had in the tenement formerly of Simon de Godild, and of all else which may accrue to the grantor in the said vill in anyway or at any future time. Sealed so that neither William, his heirs, nor his assigns may henceforth make any claim against this concession, remission and quitclaim.
Hiis testibus: Willelmo de Thelnitham, Thoma de Assewell', Willelmo Cokeman, Henrico le talyur, Alixandro de Stanton', Thoma Revel, Petro de Thorp', et aliis.

Pakenham, Thursday 17 Feb. 1290

52. Grant in heredity by Geoffrey of Thorpe (*Thorp'*) to John son of Alfred of Bardwell (*Berdewell'*) for his homage and service and for 20s of silver which he gave as entry fine, of the whole of his meadow which he had or might come to have between the pond and *Lelode*, from the mill as far as the end of the middle pond with the pasture above the pond and the whole part of the marsh in the pond of the middle mill with all that it is possible to mow (*falcari*), be there more or less, to hold and to have of the grantor and his heirs by him and his heirs or whosoever to whom he may wish to grant, sell or assign it, except for a religious house, freely and quit, well and in peace and heredity, rendering therefrom annually to the grantor and his heirs 1d at Michaelmas for all services, aids, customs, and exactions. Warranty is granted against all persons. Sealed in witness.
Hiis testibus: Henrico de Bek, Willelmo filio Roberti, Willelmo Breton', Eadmundo filio Willelmi, Adam de Suthenton', Henrico filio Willelmi de Fordiam, Willelmo ultra aquam, Galfrido le Breton', Thoma Thedred, Henrico filio Roberti, et aliis.

[Mid thirteenth century, before 1263]

53. Grant in heredity by Johanna de Boun, daughter and heir of *dominus* John of Bath (*Bathonia*), widow, to *dominus* William of Pakenham, kt, of the service [*fo. 10v*] of John Bonyard in the form of rent for a tenement that he held of her in Ixworth Thorpe, namely, 15d in rent annually at the customary terms with homages, reliefs, escheats, and all increments that may come therefrom, to hold and to have by William and his heirs or assigns, freely, quit, peaceably, in fee and heredity. Warranty is granted against all persons in perpetuity. And for this grant William gave 20s sterling in cash. Sealed in witness.
Hiis testibus: dominis Johanne de Sancto Claro, Reginaldo Peche, Johanne de Geddynge, militibus, Matheo de Thelnitham, Ricardo de Berdewell', Johanne de Berdewell', Ricardo Thannpayn, Roberto le Gynour, Petro filio Willelmi de Thelnitham, Symone de Gesselingham, Henrico le talyur, Petro de Thorp', et aliis.

Elmsett (*Elmsete*), 26 May 1296

54. Grant in heredity by Johanna de Boun, daughter and heir of *dominus* John of Bath (*Bathonia*), kt, widow, to *dominus* William of Pakenham, kt, and his heirs, of all her meadow with its appurtenances which she had in the vill of Ixworth Thorpe, to have and to hold the meadow with its appurtenances by William, his heirs and assigns, freely, quit, well and in peace, in fee and heredity perpetually. Sealed in witness.
Hiis testibus: dominis Johanne de Bellomonte, Reginaldo Peche, militibus, Matheo de Thelnitham, Roberto le Gynour, Radulfo de Berdewell', Johanne filio Willelmi de Berdewell', Radulfo le Warde, Ricardo Thannpanye, Petro de Thorp', Henrico de Ixeworth' le talyur, Petro de Redlingworth, et aliis.

Elmsett (*Elmsete*), Monday 30 Aug. 1294

55. Grant in heredity by Walter Kenne of Ixworth Thorpe to *dominus* William of Pakenham, kt, for 40s sterling, of two acres of arable land in Ixworth Thorpe, of which one and a half acres lie in the field called Broadwater (*Bradewater*) between the land of William and that of the prior of Ixworth (*Ixeworth'*), abutting at one headland on the meadow of Robert son of Ralph Symund, and half an acre lies in the field called *Ronakyrhill* between the land of William and that of John le Neve, abutting at one headland on *le Wodeweye*, be there more or less, to hold and to have by William and his heirs or assigns, freely, quit, well, peaceably, in fee and heredity. Warranty is granted against all persons in perpetuity. Sealed in witness.
Hiis testibus: domino Reginaldo Peche, milite, Willelmo de Thelnitham, Radulfo de Berdewell', Roberto ultra aquam, Simone de Gesselingham, Ricardo de Brakebregh, Roberto filio Radulfi Symund, Willelmo le Warde de Thorp', Thoma Revel, Henrico le talyur, Alixandro de Stanton', Petro de Thorp', et aliis.

[Late thirteenth century, before 1290]

56. Grant in heredity by Walter Kenne of Ixworth Thorpe to *dominus* William of Pakenham, kt, of half an acre of arable land with appurtenances in Ixworth Thorpe at the toft between the lands of William on both sides, abutting at one headland on *Thertheweye*, be there more or less, to have and to hold by William, his heirs and assigns of the capital lord of the fee by the service rightfully owed therefrom, freely, quit, [*fo. 11r*] honourably and in heredity for all services, customs and secular demands. Warranty is granted against all persons in perpetuity. And for this concession and warranty, William gave one mark of silver in cash. Sealed in witness.
Hiis testibus: Radulfo de Berdewell', Johanne filio Willelmi de eadem, Willelmo de Thelnitham, Petro filio suo, Bartholomeo de Lyvermere, Symone de Gesselingham, Roberto ultra aquam, Petro de Thorp', Roberto filio Radulfi de Thorp', et aliis.

[1290 x 1300]

57. Agreement between *dominus* William of Pakenham, kt, on the one part and John son of William of Bardwell (*Berdewell'*) on the other, whereby William granted to John six acres of land and one and a half roods of arable land and the whole heath abutting on the road called *Northernedych* between the land of William and the marsh of John as far as the heath of William, as it is measured and bounded (*pro ut mensuratum est et abundatum*), and of the foresaid land, three acres and one rood lie in the field called *Stonilond* between the land of John on both sides; one acre and three and a half roods, which were formerly of John Hereward, lie between the land of John on both sides, abutting at one headland on the said three acres and one rood; and one acre and one rood lie below the wood of William between his land and that of John, abutting at one headland on the foresaid wood, be there more or less, to hold and to have of William and his heirs by John, his heirs, and assigns or whosoever to whom he may wish to grant or sell it, freely, quit, well, peaceably and in heredity, rendering therefrom annually to William and his heirs ¼d at Michaelmas for all services, aids, all manner of suit

of court and secular demands. Warranty is granted against all persons in perpetuity. In return for this grant John granted to William all the land which William his father once purchased from William son of Walter Church (*de ecclesia*) in the field called *le Breche*; all the land which John purchased from William le Syre in the same field with the heath pertaining to it between the land and heath of William on both sides; and all the land which William, father of John, purchased from Adam of Lindsay (*Lindeye*) in the foresaid field between the land of William and the land of Alexander the cobbler (*sutor*), to hold and to have of John and his heirs by William and his heirs for a clove at Easter for all services, aids, all manner of suit of court and secular demands. Warranty is granted by both parties against all in perpetuity. Sealed respectively by each party.
Hiis testibus: Willelmo de Thelnitham, Radulfo de Berdewell', Ricardo de Suthenton', Roberto ultra aquam, Waltero le Spenser, Roberto le Spenser, Roberto de Blakebergh, Symone de Gesselingham, Nicholao Robyn, Willelmo de Willingham, Roberto de Drenkyston', Petro de Thorp', et aliis.

[Third quarter of thirteenth century, before 1283]

58. [*fo. 11v*] Agreement between *dominus* William of Pakenham, kt, on the one hand and John son of William of Bardwell (*Berdewell'*) on the other, whereby William conceded for himself and his heirs to John free common in his heath called *Spinheye* from the heath of John, as it is measured and bounded, as far as the old ditch which itself extends to another called *le Breche* as far as the marsh called *Dedemor*, for the whole of John's life so that after his death neither his heirs nor his assigns nor anyone in his name may demand or lay legal claim to the said heath. This agreement is drawn up in the form of a chirograph, sealed respectively by each party.
Hiis testibus: Willelmo de Thelnitham, Radulfo de Berdewell', Ricardo de Suthenton', Roberto ultra aquam, Symone de Gesselingham, Roberto le Syre, Petro de Thorp', Roberto de Drenkyston', et aliis.

[Third quarter of thirteenth century, before 1283]

59. Agreement between *dominus* William of Pakenham, kt, on the one hand and John son of William on the other, whereby William granted for himself and his heirs to John free common in his heath called *Spenheye* from the heath of John, as it is measured and bounded, as far as the old ditch which itself extends to another called *le Breche*, as far as the marsh called *Dedemor*, for the whole of John's life; and he granted him the right in the heath to make improvements to the common pond. After his death neither his heirs nor assigns nor anyone in his name may demand or lay legal claim in the said heath. This agreement is drawn up in the form of a chirograph, sealed respectively by each party.
Hiis testibus: Willelmo de Thelnitham, Radulfo de Berdewell', Ricardo de Suthenton', Roberto ultra aquam, Petro de Thorp', Roberto de Drenkyston', et aliis.

[Third quarter of thirteenth century, before 1283]

A repeat of no. 58, but with the added concession to make improvements to the common pond in the heath and the omission from the witness list of Simon of Gislingham and Robert le Syre.

60. Grant in heredity by John son of William of Bardwell (*Berdewell'*) to *dominus* William of Pakenham, kt, of four pieces of arable land with their appurtenances lying in the field of Ixworth Thorpe which is called *Wodecroft* between the land of William on the one side and that of John on the other, abutting at one headland on the wood of William, be there more or less, to hold and to have of the grantor and his heirs by William and his heirs or whosoever to whom he may wish to grant, sell or assign it, freely, quit, well and peaceably, in fee and heredity, rendering therefrom annually to the grantor and his heirs a clove at the feast of St Edmund [20 Nov.], for all services, aids, customs, all manner of suit of court and secular demands. Warranty is granted against all persons in perpetuity. Sealed in witness.
Hiis testibus: Willelmo de Thelnitham, Roberto le Gynur de Weston', Radulfo de Berdewell', Ricardo de Suthenton', Roberto ultra aquam, Roberto de Drenkyston', Alixandro Hubert de Thorp', et aliis.

[Third quarter of thirteenth century, before 1283]

61. Grant in heredity by William de Criketot, kt, to *dominus* William of Pakenham, kt, for his service and 20s sterling in cash, of 16d in annual rents which William of Thorpe (*Ixeworththorp'*) and his heirs and assigns, were accustomed to render to the grantor and his ancestors from the whole of the tenement that they held from him in the vill of Ixworth Thorpe, to have and to hold of the grantor and his heirs by *dominus* William and his heirs or his assigns or whosoever to whom [*fo. 12r*] he may wish to grant, sell or otherwise assign it, freely, quit, peaceably and in heredity, rendering therefrom annually to the grantor and his heirs a clove at Easter for all services, customs, all manner of suit of court, aids and secular demands. Warranty is granted against all persons in perpetuity. Sealed in witness.
Hiis testibus: domino Reginaldo Peche, Willelmo de Thelnitham, Radulfo le Blund, Radulfo de Berdewell', Johanne filio Willelmi de eadem, Ricardo de Suthenton', Symone de Gesselingham, Roberto Grehund, Willelmo le Warde, Thoma Revel, Alixandro de Stanton', Henrico le talyur, et aliis.

[Third quarter of thirteenth century, before 1283]

62. Grant in heredity by William de Mundeville (*Eadmundevile*) to William of Pakenham, for his homage and service, of a moiety of all his land and tenement which he deforced from Thomas son of William of Bardwell (*Berdewell'*) in homages, villeinages, lands, waters, woods, meadows, rights of pasture and grazing, roads, fish-ponds, and with all liberties and appurtenances pertaining to the said moiety, wherever they may be, except for the capital messuage and liberty of foldage which he has retained fully for his own use, to have and to hold by the same William, his heirs, or assigns of the grantor and his heirs, freely, quit and by inheritance, rendering therefrom annually to the grantor and his heirs one

pair of spurs out of love at Easter for all service, custom, suit of court and demand, saving forinsec service in proportion to the moiety of the said land and tenement. Warranty is granted against all persons in perpetuity. Sealed in witness.
Hiis testibus: Roberto de Wykes, Matheo de Thelnitham, Eustachio de Berningham, Thoma de Stanton', Sayero de Stanton', Galfrido de Thorp', Henrico de Berdewell', Willelmo filio Roberti, Radulfo filio Symonis, Willelmo le Syre, et aliis.

[Mid thirteenth century, before 1263]

63. Grant in heredity by Matthew of Thelnetham (*Thelnitham*), kt, to John de Verdun (*Werdun*), son of Miles de Verdun, for his homage and service, of 6d in rents in the vill of Troston taken annually from John, Goscelin and Walter his brothers, that is, at the feast of St Edmund, king and martyr [20 Nov.] 3d, and on Palm Sunday 3d, to hold and to have of the grantor and his heirs by the grantee and his heirs freely, quit, well and in peace, rendering therefrom annually to the grantor and his heirs one pair of gloves costing 1d at Michaelmas for all services, customs and demands, and if it should happen that John, Goscelin or Walter his brothers should in any way fail to make payment at the three statutory terms for the foresaid rents, then the grantee and his lawfully begotten heirs may distrain on the whole of this tenement. Warranty is granted against all persons in perpetuity.
Hiis testibus: Ricardo de Wykes, milite, domino Roberto de Norton', Johanne de Pakynham, Willelmo fratre suo, Berardo de Wattifeld, Willelmo de Thelnitham, Johanne de Stanton', Galfrido le marichal, Nicholao filio Roberti de Troston, et aliis.

[Third quarter of thirteenth century, before 1280]

64. Acknowledgement by Gilbert le Bachelor (*Bacheler*) [*fo. 12v*] and his heirs that they are bound to William of Necton (*Neketon'*) and his heirs or assigns in perpetuity for 4s of annual rent, that is, at Michaelmas 2s and at Easter 2s, and towards a scutage of 20s, when it occurs, 2s (*sic*), and for more, more, and for less, less, for a messuage and twelve acres of arable land with appurtenances in the vill of Ixworth Thorpe, which he acknowledges he holds in fee and heredity of William and his heirs by the foresaid service by reason of a sale in which John, son and heir of the late Geoffrey of Thorpe (*Thorp'*), granted it to William for his homage and for the foresaid services. Sealed so that this acknowledgement may endure in perpetuity.
Hiis testibus: Berardo de Wattsfeld, Willelmo de Thelnitham, Salomone de Ingham, Willelmo le Syre de Thorp', Petro de Ameton', Galfrido Hubert, Nicholao le Ros, Radulfo filio Symonis, et aliis.

[Third quarter of thirteenth century, before 1283]

65. Grant in heredity by Geoffrey of Thorpe (*Thorp'*) to William of Pakenham, for eight marks of silver which he gave as entry fine, of all his meadow which he

had in *Rulond* with all appurtenances and liberties, to have and to hold of the grantor and his heirs by the grantee and his heirs, freely, quit, peaceably, in fee and by inheritance, rendering therefrom annually to the grantor and his heirs 3d at Easter for all service, custom, suit of court and exaction. Warranty is granted against all, whether Christians or Jews. Sealed in witness.
Hiis testibus: Roberto de Wykes, milite, Thoma de Stanton', Radulfo de Berdewell', Henrico de Bek, Eadmundo fratre suo, Sayero de Stanton', Willelmo ultra aquam, Adam de Suthenton', Willelmo de Breton', et aliis.
[Mid thirteenth century, before 1263]

66. Quitclaim by John of Thorpe (*Thorp'*) for himself and his heirs to William his brother and his heirs or assigns of all right which he has and claim that he had or in anyway might have by virtue of inheritance in one messuage and tenement with appurtenances in Ixworth Thorpe which *dominus* William had from *dominus* Geoffrey, the grantor's father, to hold and to have by him and his heirs or his assigns, freely, quit, well, in peace, without any impediment or the imposition of a claim by the grantor or his heirs in perpetuity. Sealed in witness.
Hiis testibus: domino Roberto de Norton', domino Matheo de Thelnitham, militibus, Johanne de Stanton', Willelmo de Bottinham, Johanne de Lyvermere, Adam de Suthenton', Thoma de Ascroft, Eadmundo Tolle, Thoma Sorel, et aliis.
[Third quarter of thirteenth century, before 1280]

67. Quitclaim by John son of Geoffrey of Thorpe (*Thorp'*) for himself and his heirs to William of Pakenham and his heirs or assigns of all right which he has and claim which he had or might have by virtue of inheritance from Geoffrey, the grantor's father, in Ixworth Thorpe, namely, in messuages, lands and tenements, woods, meadows, pastures, herbages, ponds, rents, and in all places with all liberties and claims which pertain to the tenement, to hold and to have by him and his heirs or assigns, freely, quit, wholly, well and in peace without impediment or the imposition of a claim by the grantor or his assigns. Sealed in witness.
Hiis testibus: domino Roberto de Norton', domino Matheo de Thelnitham, militibus, Johanne de Stanton', Willelmo de Botynham, Johanne de Lyvermere, Adam de Suthenton', Thoma de Ascroft, Willelmo Arnald, Eadmundo Tolle, Thoma Sorel, et aliis.
[Late thirteenth – early fourteenth century, before 1302]

68. [*fo. 13r*] Grant in heredity by William of Thelnetham (*Thelnitham*) to *dominus* William of Pakenham, kt, for his service and for £8 10s sterling in cash, of eight and a half acres of arable land in the vill of Ixworth Thorpe in the field called *le Breche*, of which seven acres lie between the lands of Ixworth Priory on both sides, abutting at one headland on the land of John le Syre, and one and a half acres lie between the land which Peter of Thorpe (*Thorp'*) holds and the common pasture, abutting at one headland on the land of the said William, be there more or less, to hold and to have of the grantor and his heirs by *dominus* William and his heirs or assigns, freely, quit, well, peaceably and by inheritance,

rendering therefrom annually to the capital lord of the fee the due and customary service and to the grantor and his heirs a clove at Easter for all services, aids, customs, all manner of suit of court and secular demands. Warranty is granted against all persons in perpetuity. Sealed in witness.
Hiis testibus: Johanne filio Willelmi de Berdewell', Radulfo de Berdewell', Roberto ultra aquam, Ricardo de Suthenton', Nicholao Robyn, Galfrido le marichal, Willelmo de Willingham, Thoma Revel, Henrico le talyur, Petro de Thorp' et aliis.

[Third quarter of thirteenth century, before 1283]

69. Grant in heredity by John Baldwin (*Baldewyne*) of Ixworth (*Ixeworth'*) to *dominus* William of Pakenham, kt, for his service and 20s of silver in cash, of three acres of arable land in the vill of Ixworth Thorpe, of which one acre lies in the field called *Schamelocis* beside the land of William, and half an acre lies at *Gorehil* beside the land of Simon of Gislingham (*Gesselingham*), be there more or less, to hold and to have of the grantor and his heirs by William and his heirs or whosoever to whom he may wish to grant, sell or otherwise assign it, freely, quit, well, peaceably, in heredity, rendering therefrom annually to the grantor and his heirs a clove at Easter for all services, aids and secular demands. Warranty is granted against all persons in perpetuity. Sealed in witness.
Hiis testibus: domino Willelmo de Thelnitham, Radulfo de Berdewell', Symone de Gesselingham, Petro de Thorp', et aliis.

[Late thirteenth century, before 1290]

70. Grant in heredity by Geoffrey Hardyng of Thetford (*Theford*) to William of Pakenham, for his service and for 60s of silver which he gave as entry fine, of three acres of his land in the vill of Ixworth Thorpe with all its liberties and appurtenances, without any reservation, lying beside the wood of William towards the east, to have and to hold by William and his heirs or assigns, freely, quit, peaceably and in heredity, rendering therefrom annually to the grantor and his heirs 2d at Michaelmas and towards a scutage of 20s, ½d, and thus whether it is higher or lower, for all service, custom, suit of court, exaction and demand. Warranty is granted [*fo. 13v*] against all. Sealed in witness.
Hiis testibus: Henrico de Berdewell', Eadmundo fratre suo, Willelmo filio Roberti, Thoma de Stanton', Johanne de Stanton', Johanne de Pakynham, Adam de Suthenton', Roberto ultra aquam, Willelmo le Breton', Waltero de Herdford, et aliis.

[Third quarter of thirteenth century, before 1280]

71. Grant in heredity by William son of Robert le Syre of Ixworth Thorpe to Thomas son of Agnes le Palmere of Pakenham of three roods of arable land in Ixworth Thorpe lying in the field called *Boysdych* between the land of Robert le Syre and the pasture called *Suthheyt*, abutting at one headland on the foresaid pasture and at the other headland on the land of Robert, be there more or less, to have and to hold of the capital lord of the fee by Thomas and his heirs or assigns,

freely, quit, and in heredity, rendering therefrom annually to the capital lord ½d at Michaelmas for all services and secular demands. Warranty is granted against all persons in perpetuity. And for this concession, grant, and warranty, Thomas gave one mark of silver in cash. Sealed in witness.
Hiis testibus: Radulfo de Berdewell', Johanne filio Willelmi de eadem, Roberto ultra aquam, Petro de Thelnitham, Symone de Gesselingham, Roberto filio Radulfi de Thorp', Waltero Kenne de eadem, Willelmo le Warde, Johanne Louwyne, Johanne le Syre, Johanne de Hindycle, et aliis.

[1290 x 1300]

72. Grant in heredity by William le Warde of Ixworth Thorpe to Thomas of Pakenham and Alice his wife, for a certain sum of money in cash, of three and a half acres of arable land with appurtenances lying in the field of Ixworth Thorpe called *le Breche* between the lands of Thomas on both sides, of which one head-land is on the grantor's land and the other on the land of Walter Kenne, to have and to hold by Thomas, Alice and Thomas's heirs or his assigns of the capital lords of the fees by the due and customary service. Warranty is granted against all persons in perpetuity. Sealed in witness.
Hiis testibus: Waltero Kenne, Roberto filio Radulfi, Johanne Louwyn, Nicholao le Syre, Roberto Atehil, et aliis.

Ixworth Thorpe, Thursday 12 March 1310

73. Grant in heredity by William son of John of Great Livermere (*Lyvermere Magna*) to *dominus* William of Pakenham, kt, of 2s in annual rents which Alexander le Fever was accustomed to render for the tenement which he held from the grantor in Honington (*Huneghton'*), and 7d in annual rents which Gilbert le Milner was accustomed to render for two acres of land which he held from the grantor in Ixworth Thorpe, and also 6d in annual rents which Simon of Gislingham (*Gesselingham*) was accustomed to render for two acres which Nicholas of Troston (*Stroston'*), chaplain, held of the grantor's fee in the foresaid vill of Ixworth Thorpe, with homages, wardships, reliefs, escheats, forinsec service, that is to the scutage of the lord king when it occurs as much as pertains to this land, and all other renders from all the tenements forenamed when they occur, to have and to receive (*habendum et percipiendum*) from the foresaid Alexander, Gilbert and Simon and their heirs or assigns or from whosoever may hold the foresaid in Honington (*Hunegheton'*) and Ixworth Thorpe by William, his heirs, or assigns, freely, [*fo. 14r*] quit and by inheritance, for all services, customs, aids and secular demands. Warranty is granted against all persons in perpetuity. And for this concession, grant, and warranty William gave 20s in cash. Sealed in witness.
Hiis testibus: Radulfo de Berdewell', Johanne filio Willelmi de eadem, Roberto filio Radulfi de Thorp', Willelmo le Warde, Roberto de Blakebregh, Petro de Thorp', et aliis.

[Late thirteenth century, before 1300]

74. Grant in heredity by William of Willingham (*Wilyngham*) to *dominus* William of Pakenham, kt, for his service and four and a half acres of arable land with appurtenances which he gave in exchange, of four and a half acres of arable land in the vill of Ixworth Thorpe, of which one piece lies between the wood formerly of Geoffrey of Thorpe (*Thorp'*), abutting at one headland on the foresaid road (*predictam viam*)[a], and one piece in the field beside *Thorpepond* beside the land formerly of Ralph Cassamerre, and one piece lies beside *le Wodeweye*, abutting at one headland on the land formerly of Geoffrey of Thorpe, and one piece lies at *Longehemdlond* beside the land of Galiena of Thorpe, abutting at one headland on the land of Ralph Symund, be there more or less, to hold and to have of the grantor and his heirs by *dominus* William, his heirs or assigns, freely, quit, well, peaceably and by inheritance, rendering therefrom annually to the grantor and his heirs a clove at the feast of St Edmund, king and martyr [10 Nov.], for all services, aids, all manner of suit of court and secular demands. Warranty is granted against all persons in perpetuity. Sealed in witness.
Hiis testibus: Willelmo de Thelnitham, Radulfo de Berdewell', Ricardo de Suthenton', Roberto ultra aquam, Roberto de Rekynghal, Symone de Gesselingham, et aliis.

[Third quarter of thirteenth century, before 1283]

a Which 'predictam viam' is not made clear.

75. Grant in heredity by John son of Robert Newman (*le Neweman*) of Ixworth Thorpe to *dominus* William of Pakenham, kt, of the whole of his messuage with buildings in the vill of Ixworth Thorpe lying beside the land of William, abutting at one headland on the common pasture of Ixworth Thorpe, to have and to hold by William and his heirs and assigns of the capital lords of the fee by the due and customary service. Warranty is granted against all persons in perpetuity. For this concession, grant, and warranty, William gave 20s sterling in cash. Sealed in witness.
Hiis testibus: Radulfo de Berdewell', Johanne filio Willelmi de eadem, Roberto ultra aquam de eadem, Eadmundo le Spenser, Symone de Gesselingham, Waltero Kenne, Willelmo le Warde, et aliis.

[1290 x 1300]

76. Grant in heredity by Alexander son of Adam le smyth of Ixworth Thorpe to *dominus* William of Pakenham, kt, for his service and one mark of silver in cash, of one acre of arable land in the vill of Ixworth Thorpe in the field therein called *le Breche* between the lands of William on both sides, abutting at one headland on *Northenedych* and the other on the pasture called *Spynheth*, be there more or less, to hold and to have of the grantor and his heirs by William and his heirs or whosoever to whom he may wish to grant, sell or otherwise assign it, freely, quit, well, peaceably and in heredity, rendering therefrom annually to the grantor and his heirs a clove at Easter for all services, aids, all manner of suit of court and demands. Warranty is granted against all persons in perpetuity. Sealed in witness.
Hiis testibus: Willelmo de Thelnitham, Johanne filio Willelmo de Berdewell',

[*fo. 14v*] Ricardo de Suthenton', Roberto ultra aquam, Roberto de Rekynghal', Radulfo Symund, Ricardo de Bernham, et aliis.

[Third quarter of thirteenth century, before 1283]

77. Quitclaim by Ralph Skiwyn of Honington (*Hunegeton'*) for himself and his heirs or assigns to *dominus* William of Pakenham, kt, his heirs and assigns, of all right which he has and claim which he might have by virtue of inheritance in two acres of arable land which William Skywyn his brother held of William in the field of Honington, abutting at one headland on *Passewong*, so that neither Ralph nor his heirs nor anyone in their name may henceforth demand any right or claim in the foresaid two acres of land. And for this concession, remission, and quitclaim, William gave one mark of silver in cash. Sealed in witness.
Hiis testibus: Willelmo de Thelnitham, Radulfo de Berdewell', Johanne de Berdewell', Ricardo de Suthenton', et aliis.

[Third quarter of thirteenth century, before 1283]

78. Grant in heredity by William son of William of Shimpling (*Schymplinge*) to *dominus* William of Pakenham, kt, for 2s sterling in cash, of 1d in annual rent taken from John Newman (*le Neweman*), and 1d in annual rent taken from Walter le Bor, for two messuages which they held from the grantor in the vill of Ixworth Thorpe, to have and to hold of the grantor and his heirs by *dominus* William and his heirs or assigns with homages, wardships, reliefs, escheats and all other appurtenances that pertain to the said rents, freely, quit, well, peaceably and by inheritance, rendering therefrom annually to the grantor and his heirs a clove at the feast of St Edmund, king and martyr [20 Nov.], for all services, aids and demands. Warranty is granted against all persons in perpetuity. Sealed in witness.
Hiis testibus: Johanne filio Willelmi de Berdewell', Roberto ultra aquam, Ricardo de Suthenton', Roberto de Drenkyston', Radulfo filio Symonis de Gesselingham, Willelmo de Willingham, et aliis.

Pakenham, 7 Dec. 1280

79. Agreement between John son of William of Bardwell (*Berdewell'*) on the one hand and Thomas son of *dominus* William of Pakenham, kt, and Alice his wife on the other, whereby John granted to Thomas and Alice his wife a moiety of his water mill called *le Meldilmelne* and a moiety of the toll (*tolneti*) that comes with the foresaid mill in the vill of Ixworth Thorpe with all profits that pertain to the moiety, to have and to hold by Thomas, Alice, and their lawfully begotten heirs. Warranty is granted against all persons in perpetuity, saving to John and his heirs one moiety of the fishery that pertains to the said mill; and the other moiety of the fishery that pertains to the foresaid mill shall remain to Thomas, Alice, and their lawfully begotten heirs, on condition that neither John his heirs shall be held to nor may warrant. In return for this concession and grant Thomas is to have his mill called *le Hemyrmelne* levelled so that neither he nor Alice nor anyone for them may henceforth have it in any way rebuilt. And if the said mill is rebuilt by Thomas or Alice or their lawfully begotten heirs or by

anyone else, this concession and grant is to be held null and void; and in this event, it may be lawful for John and his heirs to recover and retain wholly and in perpetuity all the profits in his mill called *le Midilmelne* with appurtenances without objection [*fo. 15r*] or claim by Thomas, Alice and their heirs. And John on the one hand and Thomas and Alice on the other will undertake equal shares in the maintenance of the mill for their common use, and will take an equal share of the income from the mill. And if because of the negligence of John or Thomas and Alice or their heirs maintenance and repairs of the mill are not undertaken when necessary in part or in whole, then the other party and his heirs may lawfully and in the way forewritten and by the view and testimony of four law-worthy men (*fidedignorum*) from the vills of Bardwell (*Berdewell'*) and Ixworth Thorpe, from the profits of the mill, order suitable repairs, and the other party shall fully reimburse him. Sealed in witness with the seals of John, Thomas and Alice.
Hiis testibus: Ricardo de Wykes, Henrico de Berdewell', Johanne de Suthenton', Petro de Thorp' Waltero Kenne, Roberto filio Radulfi, Roberto Atehil', et aliis.

Ixworth Thorpe, Sunday 8 Jan. 1307

The original survives as BL Harleian Charter 46 A 27, bottom portion of a chirograph, 200mm wide x 160mm, two tags but both seals missing.

80. Grant in heredity by Nicholas son of Walter Robyn of Troston (*Stroston'*), chaplain, to Thomas Palmere of Pakenham of two acres of land in Ixworth Thorpe lying in the field called *Schamelocys* between the land of *dominus* William of Pakenham on the one side and that of William Cute on the other, and of one toft formerly of Walter son of Walter de Dale lying in the same vill between the land of Thomas Toffay on the one side and that of William Binchard on the other, be there more or less, to have and to hold of the capital lords in chief by Thomas and his heirs or assigns, freely, quit, well, peaceably and in heredity, rendering therefrom annually to the same capital lords of the fees the due and customary service. Warranty is granted against all persons in perpetuity. And for this grant, concession, and warranty, Thomas gave four marks of silver in cash. Sealed in witness.
Hiis testibus: dominis Willelmo de Pakynham, Reginaldo Peche, militibus, Radulfo de Berdewell', Symone de Gesselingham, Roberto de Drenkyston', Petro de Thorp', Alixandro de Stanton', et aliis.

[1290 x 1300]

81. Notification by Robert son of Ralph of Thorpe that he and his heirs are obligated to Thomas son of William of Pakenham, kt, and his heirs for all lands which Thomas gave him in exchange, to payment of an annual rent of 6d of silver to Thomas and his heirs, in equal instalments at Michaelmas and Easter, so that if they fail to make the payments in part or in whole, then, it may be lawful for Thomas and his heirs to distrain and take reparations on the said land until he has taken enough for the foresaid rents. Sealed in witness.

Tuesday 21 Nov. 1307

82. Quitclaim by William Warde of Ixworth Thorpe for himself and his heirs to Thomas son of William [*fo. 15v*] of Pakenham, kt, and his heirs, of all right which he has and claim which he had or in anyway might have by any title in a heath called *Spenheth* in the vill of Ixworth Thorpe, so that neither William nor his heirs nor anyone in their name may henceforth have any right or claim in the foresaid heath in perpetuity. Sealed in witness.
Hiis testibus: Petro de Thelnitham, Roberto le Talyur de Ixeworth', Roberto de Lehil' de Berdewell', et aliis.

Tuesday 21 Nov. 1307

83. Grant in heredity by John Lewin (*Lewyn*) of Ixworth Thorpe to *dominus* William of Pakenham and the lady Johanna his wife of one acre of arable land and pasture lying in Ixworth Thorpe in the field called *Sutholm* between the land of William on the one side and that of Simon of Gislingham (*Gesselingham*) on the other, be there more or less, to have and to hold by William and Johanna and William's heirs of the capital lord of the fee by due and customary service, freely, peaceably and by inheritance, for all services and secular demands. Warranty is granted against all persons in perpetuity. Sealed in witness.
Hiis testibus: Radulfo de Berdewell', Johanne filio Willelmi, Roberto de Drenkyston', et aliis.

[1290 x 1300]

84. Grant in heredity by Hubert Bacon, kt, to William of Pakenham, for twenty-six marks of silver which he gave as entry fine, of all the land and tenement with all liberties and appurtenances which he had in the vill of Ixworth Thorpe by the grant of Peter his son, without any reservation, to hold and to have by William and his heirs or whosoever to whom he may wish to grant, sell or assign it, freely, quit and by inheritance, rendering therefrom annually to the capital lords of the fee for the grantor and his heirs as much forinsec service as pertains to the said land for all services, customs, suit of court and demands. Warranty is granted against all persons in perpetuity. Sealed in witness.
Hiis testibus: Henrico de Berdewell', Thoma de Stanton', Galfrido de Thorp', Willelmo le Syre, Willelmo filio Roberti de Berdewell', Symone de Henton', et aliis.

[Mid thirteenth century, before 1263]

85. Grant in heredity by William son of Walter Church (*ad ecclesiam*) of Ixworth Thorpe to William of Pakenham, for his service and for six marks of silver which he gave as entry fine, of his messuage which he had in the vill of Ixworth Thorpe with the whole croft, and of one piece of his land in the middle of the vill lying towards Troston (*Stroston'*) between the land which was of Henry Sterre and that of Martin of Sapiston (*Sapiston'*); and of one piece lying near Broadwater (*Bradwater*) between the land of Ralph son of Simon and the free land of the church of Ixworth Thorpe; and of the homage and service of Gilbert le Wever for one and a half acres which he held from the grantor by the service of 1d paid in

full at Easter and towards a scutage of 20s, 1½d, and for more, more, and for less, less; and of the homage and service of William le Syre son of Peter for half an acre of land which he held from the grantor by the service of 1d paid in full at Michaelmas and towards a scutage of 20s, ½d, and for more, more, and for less, less; and of the homage and service of Walter the chaplain of Ixworth Thorpe for an acre which he held by the service of 1d paid in full at Michaelmas and for any scutage, 2d, whether it is higher or lower; and of the homage and service of William son of Geoffrey le Syre for one and a half roods of land which he held from the grantor by the service of ¼d paid in full at Michaelmas and towards a scutage of 20s, ¼d, and for more, more, and for less, less; and of the homage and service of Robert *ultra aquam* of Bardwell (*Berdewell*) for one and a third acres which he held from the grantor by the service of ¼d paid in full at Michaelmas and towards a scutage of 20s, 2d, and for more, more, and for less, less; [*fo. 16r*] and of the homage and service of Geoffrey Hubert for an acre of land which he held from the grantor by the service of 1½d, paying 1d at Michaelmas and ½d at Easter, and towards a scutage of 20s, 1d, and for more, more, and for less, less; and of the homage and service of Ralph son of Simon for three [*blank*][a] which he held from the grantor by the service of 1d at Michaelmas and towards a scutage of 20s, 1d, and for more, more, and for less, less; and of the homage and service of Peter the chaplain of Troston (*Stroston'*) for a half acre of land which he held from the grantor by the service of 1d at Michaelmas and towards a scutage of 20s, 1d, and for more, more, and for less, less; and of the homage and service of Nicholas Scot of Troston for a half acre of land which he held from the grantor by the service of ½d at the feast of the Nativity of John the Baptist [24 June] and towards a scutage of 20s, ½d, and for more, more, and for less, less; and of the homage and service of Walter Robyn for one and a half roods of land which he held from the grantor by the service of ½d at Easter and towards a scutage of 20s, ½d, and for more, more, and for less, less; and of the homage and service of Ralph the clerk of Honington (*Huneton'*) for half a rood of land which he held from the grantor by the service of ¼d at Michaelmas; and of the homage and service of Nicholas the smith (*faber*) of Honington (*Hunegton'*) for half a rood of land which he held from the grantor by the service of ¼d every two years (*per duos annos*) at Michaelmas; and of the homage and service of William Lewin (*Lewyn*) for a half acre of land which he held from the grantor by the service of ½d at Michaelmas and towards a scutage of 20s, ½d, and for more, more, and for less, less; and of the homage and service of Walter Wrakesham for a half rood of land which he held by paying 1d towards a scutage of 20s, and for more, more, and for less, less; and of the homage and service of Walter Dust for an acre of land which he held from the grantor by paying 1d towards a scutage of 20s, and for more, more, and for less, less; and of the homage and service of Nicholas le Rus for a half acre of land which he held from the grantor by paying ½d towards a scutage of 20s, and for more, more, and for less, less; and of the homage and service of Robert le Milner for a certain messuage which he held from the grantor by paying ½d towards a scutage of 20s, and for more, more, and for less, less; with all liberties and with all escheats and appurtenances which may accrue to the grantor without any reservation, to have and to hold by the same William and his heirs or his assigns from the grantor and his heirs or his assigns, freely, quit, well, peaceably and in heredity, rendering therefrom annually for the grantor

and his heirs or his assigns to the capital lords of the fees the due and customary service, namely that which pertains to the said tenements, for all service, custom, exaction, suit of court and demand. Warranty is granted against everyone. Sealed in witness.
Hiis testibus: Johanne fratre dicti Willelmi, Henrico de Berdewell', Eadmundo fratre suo, Willelmo filio Roberti, Adam de Suthenton', Galfrido de Thorp', Johanne de Pakynham, et aliis.

[Mid thirteenth century, before 1263]

a The manuscript omits the land measurement.

86. Grant in heredity by Honghredis de Ayngos to *dominus* William of Pakenham and the lady Johanna his wife of two acres and a rood of arable land in the field of Ixworth Thorpe, of which one acre and one rood lie in the field called *Mikylferlong* between the lands of William on both sides, abutting at one headland on *le Wodeweye*, and three roods lie between the road leading towards *Brodyng* and the land of William, abutting at one headland on *le Wodeweye* and the other on the land of William, be there more or less, to have and to hold of the capital lords of the fees by William and Johanna and the heirs or assigns of William, freely, quit, well, in peace, in fee and heredity by the due and customary service. Warranty is granted against all persons in perpetuity. And in return for this concession, grant, confirmation and warranty, [*fo. 16v*] William gave 40s sterling in cash. Sealed in witness.
Hiis testibus: Radulfo de Berdewell, Johanne filio Willelmi de eadem, Roberto ultra aquam, Johanne de Suthenton', Roberto filio Radulfi, Symone de Gesselingham, Henrico le talyur, Petro de Thorp', et aliis.

[1290 x 1300]

87. Grant in heredity by Adam of Ingham to *dominus* William of Pakenham, kt, for his service and 10s of silver in cash, of the homage and service of Lawrence son of Fulk of Pakenham, and of the homage and service of Alured of Drinkstone (*Drenkyston*), and of the homage and service of Robert of Drinkstone, and of the homage and service of Robert *ultra aquam* of Bardwell (*Berdewell'*), namely, 6d a year and the rents in which they are obligated to the grantor each year for the tenement which William of Pakenham formerly acquired from Salomon the grantor's father, to hold and to have the said rents with homages, wardships, reliefs, escheats and all other appurtenances which may pertain to the tenement of the grantor and his heirs by William and his heirs or assigns, freely, quit, well, peaceably and by inheritance, rendering therefrom annually to the grantor and his heirs a clove at Easter for all services, aids, all manner of suit of court and secular demands. Warranty is granted against all persons in perpetuity. Sealed in witness.
Hiis testibus: Willelmo de Thelnitham, Radulfo de Berdewell, Symone de Gesselingham, Nicholao de Stanton, Petro de Thorp', et aliis.

[Late thirteenth century, before 1290]

88. Grant in heredity by William son of Henry Steure of Ixworth Thorpe to William of Pakenham, for 3s of silver which he gave as entry fine, of a piece of marsh which he had in *Dedemor* in the parish of Ixworth Thorpe lying near the marsh which was formerly of Robert Newman (*le Neweman*) towards the west, with all its appurtenances and liberties without reservation, to have and to hold by William and his heirs or his assigns of the grantor and his heirs, freely, quit, well, peaceably and by inheritance, rendering therefrom annually to the grantor and his heirs a clove at Michaelmas for all service, custom, exaction and demand. Warranty is granted against all persons in perpetuity. Sealed in witness.
Hiis testibus: Ricardo Dikeman de Fuldon', Rogero filio suo, Willelmo filio Roberti, Roberto ultra aquam, Johanne Scot, et aliis.

[Third quarter of thirteenth century, before 1280]

89. Grant in heredity by Robert Puttok of Ixworth (*Ixeworth*) to *dominus* William of Pakenham, kt, for his service and for 20s sterling which he gave as entry fine, of two and a half acres of marsh[a] in the vill of Ixworth Thorpe called *Dedemor* between the marsh of William on the one side and that of William le Warde on the other, be there more or less, to have and to hold of the grantor and his heirs by William and his heirs or his assigns or whosoever to whom he may wish to grant, sell or otherwise assign it, freely, quit, well, in peace, honourably and by inheritance, rendering therefrom annually to the grantor and his heirs a clove at Easter for all services, customs, all manner of suit of court, aids and demands. Warranty is granted against all persons in perpetuity. Sealed in witness.
Hiis testibus: domino Reginaldo Peche, Willelmo de Thelnitham, Petro de Thorp', Alixandro de Stanton', et aliis.

[Late thirteenth century, before 1290]

a 'terre' underlined for cancellation.

90. Grant in heredity by Richard of Barnham (*Bernham*) of Ixworth Thorpe to *dominus* William of Pakenham, kt, for 20s[a] sterling in cash, of three roods of arable land in the vill of Ixworth Thorpe in the field called *le Rokyslond* beside the land of William, abutting at one headland on the land of John de Londismere, and of an acre of land in the field called *le Breche* beside the land of William, with 1d [*fo. 21r*][b] in annual rent which the grantor was accustomed to take from Cecily of Brakelond for the land called *le Redeakyr* with all its appurtenances, to hold and to have of the grantor and his heirs by William and his heirs or assigns, freely, quit, well, peaceably and by inheritance, rendering therefrom annually to the grantor and his heirs a clove at Easter for all services, aids and secular demands. Warranty is granted against all persons in perpetuity. Sealed in witness.
Hiis testibus: Willelmo de Thelnitham, Galfrido le mareschal, Roberto ultra aquam, Radulfo filio Symonis, Symone de Gesselingham, Willelmo le Syre, Johanne le Syre, et aliis.

[Late thirteenth century, before 1290]

a 'vinginti vinginti' in error.
b The cartulary was misbound sometime after it was compiled but before it was numbered.

91. Grant in heredity by Ralph of London to William of Pakenham, for his service and for 40s of silver which he gave as entry fine, of three acres of arable land with all its liberties and appurtenances in Ixworth Thorpe which he had by the grant of Cecily of Barnham (*Bernham*), lying near the land of William on the southern part, abutting at one headland on the king's highway leading from Ixworth to the church of Ixworth Thorpe, and of 2d in annual rents which the grantor was accustomed to take from Ralph son of Simon and Ellis Lewin (*Leuwyn*) for a tenement which they held from him in the said vill of Ixworth Thorpe with their homage and with all escheats which may accrue by any reason to him or his heirs from the said tenement without reservation, to have and to hold by William and his heirs or his assigns of the grantor and his heirs, freely, quit, peaceably and by inheritance, rendering therefrom annually for the grantor and his heirs to the lords of the fee the service that pertains to the land and tenement. Warranty is granted against all. Sealed in witness.
Hiis testibus: Henrico de Berdewell, Eadmundo fratre suo, Willelmo filio Roberti de Berdewell, Adam de Suthenton', Henrico de Suthenton', Willelmo le Syre, et aliis.

[Third quarter of thirteenth century, before 1280]

92. Grant in heredity by William le Celer of Honington (*Honnegton'*) to *dominus* William of Pakenham, kt, for his service and for 30s of silver which he gave as entry fine, of two and a half acres of arable land with their appurtenances in the field of Ixworth Thorpe which is called *le Longhemdlond* between the land of Margaret of Thorpe (*Thorp'*), which she holds as her dower, on the one side and that of Philip le Ferour on the other, abutting at one headland on the field which is called *le Stubbinge*, be there more or less, to have and to hold of the grantor and his heirs by William and his heirs or whosoever to whom he may wish to grant, sell or assign it, freely, quit, well, peaceably, in fee and heredity, rendering therefrom annually to the grantor and his heirs a clove for all services, aids, customs, suits of court and demands. Warranty is granted against all persons in perpetuity. Sealed in witness.
Hiis testibus: Radulfo de Berdewell, Johanne filio Willelmi, Ricardo de Suthenton', Roberto ultra aquam, Radulfo filio Symonis, et aliis.

[Third quarter of thirteenth century, before 1283]

93. Agreement between Thomas son of William of Pakenham, kt, on the one hand and Walter Kenne of Ixworth Thorpe on the other, whereby Thomas conceded and gave in exchange to Walter five roods of land with appurtenances in Ixworth Thorpe, of which three roods of land lie in the field called *le Hechtakres* between the land of the prior of Ixworth (*Ixeworth'*) on the one side and that of Matilda le Ros on the other, abutting at one headland on *Dustysdygh*, and half an acre of land with appurtenances lies in the field called *Schortebreche* between the land of Matilda le Ros on the one side and that of Walter on the other, abutting at one headland on the common pasture of Ixworth Thorpe, to have and to hold by him and his heirs and assigns of the capital lords of the fees, freely, quit, wholly, well, peaceably, in fee and heredity, by the due and customary

service; and Walter conceded and in exchange gave to Thomas five roods of land with appurtenances lying in the field called *Kempisdyghc* between the lands of Thomas on both sides, abutting at one headland on the land of the prior of Ixworth (*Ixeworth'*), and half an acre of land with appurtenances lying in the field called *Kempistyghc* between the lands of Thomas on both sides, abutting at [*fo. 21v*] one headland on the land of Thomas, and one rood of land lying in the field called *Brodynge* between the lands of Thomas on both sides, abutting at one headland on the land of Walter, to have and to hold by him and his heirs and assigns of the capital lords of the fee, wholly, well, peaceably, in fee and heredity by the due and customary service. Warranty is granted in perpetuity. Sealed respectively by each party.
Hiis testibus: Johanne de Berdewell, Ricardo de Wykes, Roberto Atehil' de Berdewell, et aliis.

Ixworth Thorpe, Friday 16 June 1307

94. Grant in heredity by Matilda widow of Thomas le Mayster of Ixworth (*Ixeworth'*) to *dominus* William of Pakenham, kt, for his service and five marks sterling in cash, of a messuage with its buildings and two acres of arable land with appurtenances in the croft of the same messuage with all the appurtenances that pertain to the messuage and land in the vill of Ixworth Thorpe between the land of Richard of Barnham (*Bernham*) and that of William son of Adam, to hold and to have of the grantor and her heirs by William and his heirs or assigns, freely, quit, well, peaceably and by inheritance, rendering therefrom annually to the capital lords of the fee the due and customary service and to the grantor and her heirs a clove at Easter for all aids and secular demands. Warranty is granted against all persons in perpetuity. Sealed in witness.
Hiis testibus: Willelmo de Thelnitham, Radulfo de Berdewell, Ricardo de Suthenton', Roberto ultra aquam, Willelmo de Wilingham, Ricardo de Bernham, et aliis.

[Third quarter of thirteenth century, before 1283]

95. Grant in heredity by Henry son of Nicholas of Bury St Edmunds (*Sancto Eadmundo*) to *dominus* William of Pakenham, kt, for his service and one mark of silver in cash, of an acre of arable land in the vill of Ixworth Thorpe in the field called *Stonilond* between the land of William and that of John son of William, abutting at one headland on the herbage of John, be there more or less, to have and to hold of the grantor and his heirs by William and his heirs or assigns, freely, quit, well, peaceably and by inheritance, rendering therefrom annually to the capital lords of the fee the due and customary service and to the grantor and his heirs a clove at Easter for all services, aids, all manner of suit of court and secular demands. Warranty is granted against all persons in perpetuity. Sealed in witness.
Hiis testibus: Willelmo de Thelnitham, Radulfo de Berdewell, Johanne filio Willelmi, Roberto ultra aquam, Petro de Thorp', et aliis.

[Late thirteenth century, before 1290]

96. Grant in heredity by John son of Ralph of Hepworth (*Heppeworth*) to *dominus* William of Pakenham, kt, for his service and 3s sterling in cash, of the homage and service of Robert of Shelland (*Schidlond*) of Stanton and also of 5d in annual rents which Robert was accustomed to render to the grantor each year at Michaelmas and Easter for the whole of the tenement which he held from the grantor in the vill of Stanton, to have and to hold of the grantor and his heirs by William and his heirs or assigns or whosoever to whom he may wish to grant, sell or assign it, freely, quit, in peace, and in heredity, rendering therefrom annually to the grantor and his heirs a clove at Easter for all services, customs, suits of court, aids and demands. Warranty is granted against all persons in perpetuity. Sealed in witness.
Hiis testibus: dominis Johanne de Gnetissal', Petro de Thelnitham, Willelmo de Neketon', Reginaldo Peche, militibus, Henrico filio Nicholai, Nicholao de Stanton', Thoma filio Thome, Ricardo filio Thome, Alixandro fratre eorum, Galfrido filio Johannis, Johanne Osselyn, Johanne filio suo, et aliis.

[Late thirteenth century, before 1290]

97. [*fo. 22r*] Grant in heredity by William of Thelnetham (*Thelnitham*) to *dominus* William [of Pakenham], kt, for his service and for 60s sterling in cash, of two acres and a rood of arable land in the vill of Ixworth Thorpe , of which one and a half acres lie in the field called *Scymplinghiscroft* between the land of Robert le Syre and that of Alice Dust, abutting at one headland on the messuage of Walter le Bor, and three roods of land in the same vill in the field called *le Breche* between the land of Simon of Gislingham (*Gesselingham*) and that of William Isabel, abutting at one headland on the land of Ralph son of Simon, be there more or less, to hold and to have of the grantor and his heirs by William and his heirs or assigns or whosover to whom he may wish to grant, sell or otherwise assign it, freely, quit, well, peaceably and by inheritance, rendering therefrom annually for the grantor and his heirs to William de Schymplinge and his heirs ½d at Michaelmas and to the grantor and his heirs a clove for all services, aids, all manner of suit of court and secular demands. Warranty is granted against all persons in perpetuity. Sealed in witness.
Hiis testibus: Radulfo de Berdewell', Johanne filio Willelmi de eadem, Ricardo de Suthenton', Nicholao Robyn de eadem, Petro de Thorp', et aliis.

[Third quarter of thirteenth century, before 1283]

98. Grant in heredity by Geoffrey son of John the marshal (*le marchal*) to *dominus* William of Pakenham, kt, for his service and 30s sterling in cash, of an acre of arable land in the field of Ixworth Thorpe lying between the land of John Hereward and that of Sara Ryfflay, abutting at one headland on the common pasture, be there more or less, to have and to hold of the grantor and his heirs by William and his heirs, freely, quit, well, peaceably and by inheritance, rendering therefrom annually to the grantor and his heirs a clove at Michaelmas for all services, aids and demands. Warranty is granted against all persons in perpetuity. Sealed in witness.
Hiis testibus: Willelmo de Thelnitham, Berardo de Wattisfeld, Roberto de

Weston', Johanne filio Willelmi de Berdewell', Roberto ultra aquam de eadem, et aliis.

[Late thirteenth century, before 1290]

99. Grant in heredity by Matilda widow of Thomas le Meyster to *dominus* William of Pakenham, kt, for his service and 20s sterling in cash, of an acre of arable land in the vill of Ixworth Thorpe in the field called *le Longebreche*[a] between the land of the prior of Ixworth (*Ixeworth'*) and that of William son of Adam, abutting at one headland on the land of John le Syre, be there more or less, to hold and to have of the grantor and his heirs by William and his heirs or whosoever to whom he may wish to grant, sell, or in anyway assign it, freely, quit, well, peaceably, in heredity, rendering therefrom annually to the capital lord of the fee the due and customary service and to the grantor and his heirs a clove at Easter for all services, aids, all manner of suit of court and demands. Warranty is granted against all persons in perpetuity. Sealed in witness.
Hiis testibus: Willelmo de Thelnitham, Radulfo de Berdewell', Roberto ultra aquam, Roberto de Blakebergh, Henrico cyssore, Willelmo filio Ade, Willelmo le Syre, Symone de Gesselingham, et aliis.

[Late thirteenth century, before 1290]

a 'Breche' underlined for cancellation.

100. Quitclaim by Robert *ultra aquam* of Bardwell (*Berdewell'*) for himself and his heirs to William of Pakenham of one acre of land in two pieces and half an acre of marsh in the vill of Ixworth Thorpe with all their liberties and appurtenances without any reservation, to have and to hold by William and his heirs or [*fo. 22v*] assigns of the lords of the fee by the due and customary service which pertain to the foresaid tenement in perpetuity. Sealed in witness.
Hiis testibus: Henrico de Berdewell', Eadmundo fratre suo, Willelmo Arnald, Henrico Aceforth, Willelmo le Breton', et aliis.

[Third quarter of thirteenth century, before 1280]

101. Quitclaim by John le Syre and Nicholas le Syre of Ixworth Thorpe to Thomas son of *dominus* William of Pakenham, kt, of all right and claim which they had or in anyway might henceforth have in the whole of the tenement which *dominus* William purchased from their ancestors in the vill of Ixworth Thorpe, and after the death of Margaret de Aula of a tenement which was held by her in dower from their inheritance which they occupy, to have and to hold by Thomas and his heirs or assigns of the capital lord of the fee by the due and customary service, freely, quit, well, peaceably and in heredity, so that neither John and Nicholas nor their lawful heirs may have any right or claim in the tenements with appurtenances, and for this concession, remission, and quitclaim, Thomas gave to the grantors a mark of silver in cash. Sealed in witness with their seals.

Hiis testibus: Petro de Thelnitham, Johanne filio Willelmi de Bardewell', Roberto filio Radulfi, et aliis.

Ixworth Thorpe, 8 July 1305

102. Grant in heredity by Reginald Arsyk for himself and his heirs to William of Pakenham, for his service, of all the service of William de Mundeville and his heirs for the whole fee and tenement which William de Mundeville holds of the grantor in Ixworth Thorpe with rents, reliefs, custodies, escheats, and all other things which may accrue to the grantor or his heirs, lawfully [and] hereditably, by reason of the foresaid fee and tenement, namely, from a fee of two knights, saving to the grantor and his heirs only the homage of William de Mundeville and his heirs, to have and to hold by William of Pakenham and his heirs or assigns and their heirs of the grantor and his heirs, freely, by inheritance, in perpetuity, rendering to the capital lords of the fees for the grantor and his heirs the due and customary service. Warranty is granted against all men in perpetuity. Sealed in witness.
Hiis testibus: dominis Matheo de Thelnitham, Eustachio de Wykes, Roberto de Wykes, militibus, Roberto de Norton', Thoma de Pakynham, Johanne Gloustere, Thoma de Stanton', Johanne de Stanton', et aliis.

[Late thirteenth century, before 1290]

103. Grant in heredity by William de Mundeville (*Emundevill*) to William of Pakenham, for his service, of a moiety of the whole land and tenement in the vill of Ixworth Thorpe which Thomas son of William of Bardwell (*Berdewell'*) acknowledged to be the grantor's right and returned to the grantor in the court of the lord king's itinerant justices at Cattishall (*Catteshil'*), that is in homages, villeinages, waters, woods, meadows, pastures, heaths, marshes, roads, services, and with all liberties and appurtenances pertaining to the foresaid moiety wheresoever they may be, except the capital messuage and free foldage (*libertatem falde*) which is retained for the grantor's use, to have and to hold by William and his heirs or assigns and their heirs of the grantor and his heirs, freely, quit and by inheritance in perpetuity, rendering therefrom annually to the grantor and his heirs suit of court and demand, saving forinsec service as much as it pertains to the said moiety. Warranty is granted [*fo. 23r*] against all persons in perpetuity. Sealed in witness.
Hiis testibus: Roberto de Wykes, Matheo de Thelnitham, Eustachio de Bugham, Thoma de Stanton', et aliis.

[Late thirteenth century, before 1290]

Probably after the Suffolk eyre of November 1286–February 1287 (see D. Crook, *Records of the General Eyre*, London, HMSO, 1982, 167–8).

104. Grant in heredity by Robert son of Edmund of Elveden to *dominus* William of Pakenham, kt, for his service and 40s sterling in cash, of three acres of arable land with a certain outlier (*forrea*) which William of Thorpe (*Thorp'*) gave to

Beatrice his sister in the vill of Ixworth Thorpe, of which the three acres of land lie in the field of Ixworth Thorpe between the lands of *dominus* William on both sides, abutting at one headland on *Thorpehallei pond*, and the foresaid outlier lies at the head of the land formerly of Alice Cassamerre, abutting at one headland on the messuage of Margeret de Aula and the other on the margin of the said three acres, to hold and to have of the grantor and his heirs by *dominus* William and his heirs or assigns, freely, quit, well, peaceably and by inheritance by the service of a clove paid annually at Easter for all services, aids, all manner of suit of court and secular demands. Warranty is granted against all persons in perpetuity. Sealed in witness.
Hiis testibus: Willelmo de Thelnitham, Johanne de Berdewell', Radulfo de Berdewell', Roberto ultra aquam, et aliis.

[Late thirteenth century, before 1290]

105. Grant in heredity by Hubert son of Andrew of Thorpe to William of Pakenham, for his service and for 4s of silver which he gave as entry fine, of a piece of marsh which he had in *Dedemor* and a piece of heath which he had in the vill of Ixworth Thorpe to the south of the foresaid marsh in the heath of the vill, with all their liberties and appurtenances without reservation, to have and to hold of the grantor and his heirs by the grantee and his heirs or his assigns, freely, quit, peaceably and by inheritance, rendering therefrom annually for the grantor and his heirs to the lord of the fee the service which pertains to the tenement. Warranty is granted against all. Sealed in witness.
Hiis testibus: Henrico de Berdewell', Eadmundo fratre suo, Willelmo, Roberto, Galfrido de Thorp', Radulfo filio Symonis, et aliis.

[Mid thirteenth century, before 1263]

106. Grant in heredity by John Baldwin of Ixworth (*Ixeworth'*) to *dominus* William of Pakenham, kt, for his service and half a mark of silver in cash, of an acre of arable land in the vill of Ixworth Thorpe in the field called *Sutholm* between the land of William and that of Geoffrey Crestemasse, abutting at one headland on the herbage, be there more or less, to hold and to have of the grantor and his heirs or assigns, freely, quit, well, peaceably and in heredity, rendering therefrom annually to the grantor and his heirs a clove at Michaelmas for all services, aids and secular demands. Warranty is granted against all persons in perpetuity. Sealed in witness.
Hiis testibus: Willelmo de Thelnitham, Galfrido le marychal, Roberto de Blakeberge, Willelmo de Wilyngham, Nicholao Robyn, Roberto ultra aquam, Willelmo filio Ade, Petro de Thorp', et aliis.

[Late thirteenth century, before 1290]

107. [*fo. 23v*] Grant in heredity by Thomas son of Cecily of Brakelond to *dominus* William of Pakenham, for his service and 20s of silver in cash, of an acre of arable land in the vill of Ixworth Thorpe in the field called *le Rokeslond* beside the land of William, abutting at one headland on the land of the prior of

Ixworth and the other on *le Wodeweye*, be there more or less, to hold and to have of the grantor and his heirs by William and his heirs or whosoever to whom he may wish to grant, sell or otherwise assign it, freely, quit, well, peaceably and by inheritance, rendering therefrom annually to Richard of Barnham (*Bernham*) 1d and to the grantor and his heirs a clove at Easter for all services, aids and secular demands. Warranty is granted against all persons in perpetuity. Sealed in witness.
Hiis testibus: Radulfo de Rekynhal', Roberto ultra aquam, Waltero le Spenser, Symone de Gesselingham, Ricardo de Bernham, et aliis.

[Late thirteenth century, before 1290]

108. Grant in heredity by Richard of Barnham (*Bernham*) of Ixworth Thorpe to *dominus* William of Pakenham, kt, for his service and 10s sterling in cash, of three roods of arable land in the vill of Ixworth Thorpe in the field called *Bromslede* beside the land of John le Syre, abutting at one headland on *le Wodeweye*, be there more or less, to hold and to have of the grantor and his heirs by William and his heirs or assigns, freely, quit, well, peaceably and by inheritance, rendering therefrom annually to the grantor and his heirs a clove at Easter for all services, aids, all manner of suit of court and secular demands. Warranty is granted against all persons in perpetuity. Sealed in witness.
Hiis testibus: Willelmo de Thelnitham, Johanne de Berdewell', Roberto ultra aquam, Ricardo de Suthenton', Roberto de Blakebergh, Willelmo de Wilyngham, Symone de Gesselingham, et aliis.

[Third quarter of thirteenth century, before 1283]

109. Grant in heredity by William Harding the elder of Thetford (*Theford*) to William of Pakenham, for his service and for 10s of silver in cash, of two acres of arable land in the field of Ixworth Thorpe[a] which is called *Schorelond*, lying between the land which was of William de Mundeville and that which was of Geoffrey of Barnham (*Bernham*), to hold and to have of the grantor and his heirs by the grantee and his heirs or whosoever to whom he may wish to grant, sell, bequeath or assign it, freely, quit, in fee and heredity, rendering therefrom annually for the grantor and his heirs to Geoffrey Harding of Thetford and his heirs 2d, that is at Easter 1d and at Michaelmas 1d, for all services, customs, exactions, demands and suit of court, saving the service of the lord king, that is, towards a scutage of 20s, 1d, and for more, more, and for less, less. Warranty is granted against all persons in perpetuity. Sealed in witness.
Hiis testibus: Willelmo filio Roberti de Berdewell', Eadmundo Tolle, Waltero de Herford, Galfrido de Thorp', Seman' de Willingham, et aliis.

[Mid thirteenth century, before 1263]

a 'in campo de campo de Thorp'.

110. Grant in heredity by Walter the chaplain son of William le Syre of Ixworth Thorpe to *dominus* William of Pakenham, kt, for his service and [*fo. 24r*] 10s sterling in cash, of half an acre of meadow in the vill of Ixworth Thorpe between

the messuage of William on the one side and that of the prioress of Bungay (*Bunegeye*), to hold and to have of the grantor and his heirs by William and his heirs or assigns, freely, quit, well, peaceably and in heredity, rendering therefrom annually to the grantor and his heirs a clove at Easter for all services, aids, all manner of suit of court and secular demands. Warranty is granted against all persons in perpetuity. Sealed in witness.
Hiis testibus: Willelmo de Thelnitham, Johanne filio Willelmi, Radulfo de Berdewell', Roberto ultra aquam, Roberto le Syre, Ricardo de Bernham, et aliis.

[Late thirteenth century, before 1290]

111. Grant in heredity by William Sterre of Ixworth Thorpe to John of Pakenham, rector of the church of Hawkedon (*Haukedon'*), for 30d which he gave as entry fine, of 3d of annual rents with all their appurtenances in the vill of Ixworth Thorpe and with all things which he or his heirs might by any reason acquire in the said rents, that is, from Walter le Syre, chaplain, ½d for a rood of land lying between the land of Peter de la Dale and Stephen of Honington (*Hungueton'*) which he first held from the grantor; from William brother of the same Walter ½d for a rood of land lying between the land of Adam Cande of Honington and that of Nicholas le Ros; and from Mr Hugh of Thorpe (*Thorp'*) 2d of annual rents for a certain acre of arable land lying in the field of Troston (*Stroston'*) which he held from the grantor, to have and to hold of the grantor and his heirs or assigns and their heirs, freely, quit and in heredity, rendering therefrom annually to the grantor[a] and his heirs a clove at Easter for all service, suit of court and demand. Warranty is granted against all. Sealed in witness.
Hiis testibus: Johanne de Pakynham, Willelmo fratre suo, Willelmo filio Roberti de Berdewell', Radulfo filio Symonis, et aliis.

[Third quarter of thirteenth century, before 1280]

a 'capitali' underlined for cancellation.

112. Grant in heredity by Pain de St Philibert and Iden his wife to William of Pakenham, for his homage and service, of their messuage and land which they had in the vill of Ixworth Thorpe with all its appurtenances and liberties wheresoever it may be, as in demesne lands, advowsons of churches, meadows, pastures, woods, fisheries, turf-pits, marshes, rents, homages, services, free men, villeins holding in the said villeinages with their profits and *sequelae*, and with all escheats which by right or any cause may accrue to the grantor and Iden and Iden's heirs, and with all rights which the grantor and Iden and Iden's heirs may acquire in the said tenement in whatever part of the fee, and with all things named and not named pertaining to the tenement without any reservation, to have and to hold by William and his heirs or his assigns and their heirs of the grantor and Iden and Iden's heirs in perpetuity, freely and quit, wholly, peaceably and by inheritance, rendering therefrom annually to the grantor and Iden and Iden's heirs a pair of gloves worth 1d at Michaelmas for all services, customs, suits of court, reliefs, custodies and all demands, and rendering therefrom for the grantor and Iden and Iden's heirs to the capital lords of the fees the services which pertain to

the tenement. Warranty is granted [*fo. 24v*] against all persons in perpetuity. Sealed in witness.
Hiis testibus: Roberto de Wykes, Adam de Catesthorp', Thoma de Pakynham, Roberto de Neketon', Johanne Wilandre, Thoma fratre suo, [a]Laurencio del Broke, Andrea Crok, Willelmo de Wendlesford, Willelmo de Wendelesword, Johanne de Pakeham, Ricardo de Boyland, Willelmo de Bernham, Radulfo filio Simonis et aliis.

[Late thirteenth century, before 1290]

a The following names are added to the cartulary copy by the original, which survives as BL Additional Charter 5926, single-sheet original, 217mm wide x 110mm, seal and tag missing.

112a. Final concord made in the *curia regis* at Westminster on 20 January 1256 before Roger de Thurkilby and John of Wyville, justices, between William of Pakenham, plaintiff, and Pain de St Philibert and Isold his wife, defendants, relating to a messuage and sixty acres of land with appurtenances in Ixworth Thorpe, whereof the plea was to warrant the charter which was between them in the same court, namely that Pain and Isold acknowledged that of the messuage and sixty acres of land Robert le Blund holds for a set term of years, thirty acres of land are William's by right of the grant of Pain and Isold with its appurtenances, as in diverse homages and services of free men, villeinages, wardships, reliefs, escheats, meadows, pastures, woods and other things pertaining to the messuage and land without reservation, to have and to hold by William and his heirs of Pain and Isold and Isold's heirs in perpetuity, rendering therefrom each year one pair of white gloves worth 1d at Easter for all services, suit of court, wardships, reliefs, aids, customs and exactions, and to the capital lords of the fee all other services pertaining to the messuage and land. Warranty is granted against all men in perpetuity. And for this acknowledgement, warranty, quittance, defence and final concord, William gave to Pain and Isold one unmewed sparrowhawk. This litigation was done in the presence of Robert, who acknowledged that he had no right in the said thirty acres beyond the said term.

PRO, CP 25/1/214/24 no. 232; approx. 134 x 150mm

113. Grant in heredity by William of Willingham (*Wilingham*) to *dominus* William of Pakenham, kt, for his service and 40s sterling in cash, of one and a half acres of arable land with appurtenances in the vill of Ixworth Thorpe in the field called *Wetelond* between the land of *dominus* William on both sides, abutting at one headland on the road leading to the church of Ixworth Thorpe, be there more or less, to hold and to have of the grantor and his heirs by *dominus* William and his heirs or assigns, freely, quit, well, peaceably, in fee and heredity, rendering therefrom annually to the grantor and his heirs a clove at the feast of King Edmund [20 Nov.] for all services, aids, customs, all manner of suit of court and secular demands. Warranty is granted against all persons in perpetuity. Sealed in witness.
Hiis testibus: Willelmo de Thelnitham, Radulfo de Berdewell', Johanne filio

Willelmi, Ricardo de Suthenton', Roberto ultra aquam, Symone de Gesselingham, et aliis.

[Third quarter of thirteenth century, before 1283]

114. Grant in heredity by William le Breton of Bardwell (*Berdewell'*) to William of Pakenham of the whole of his meadow which he had in *Broding* in the vill of Ixworth Thorpe beside *Brechelisbosk*, for 20s of silver which he gave as entry fine, to have and to hold by William and his heirs or assigns of the grantor and his heirs, freely, quit, peaceably and by inheritance, rendering therefrom annually to the grantor and his heirs 2½d, that is, at Easter 1¼d and at Michaelmas 1¼d, for all service, custom, suit of court and exaction. Warranty is granted against all persons. Sealed in witness.
Hiis testibus: Henrico de Berdewell', Thoma de Stanton', Johanne de Stanton', Sayero de Stanton', Roberto de Norton', Thoma de Pakynham, et aliis.

[Late thirteenth century, before 1290]

115. Grant in heredity by Cecily of Brakelond and Thomas her son, chaplain, to *dominus* William of Pakenham, kt, and Johanna his wife, of three roods of land in Ixworth Thorpe lying in the field called *le Toftis* between the lands of William on both sides, be there more or less, to hold and to have by William, Johanna, and William's heirs of the capital lord of the fee by the due and customary service, freely, peaceably and by inheritance, for all services, aids and secular demands. Warranty is granted against all persons in perpetuity. In witness etc.

[1290 x 1305]

116. [*fo. 17r*] Grant in heredity by John son of William Louwyn of Ixworth Thorpe to *dominus* William of Pakenham, kt, and the lady Johanna his wife, for 50s of silver which they gave in cash, of two acres of arable land in the vill of Ixworth Thorpe between the road which is called Outgate (*le Utgaut*) and the land of Simon of Gislingham (*Gesselingham*), abutting at one headland on the land of William and at the other on the herbage of William which is called *Broding*, be there more or less, to hold and to have of the capital lord of the fee by William and Johanna and William's heirs, freely, quit, well, peaceably, in fee and heredity by the due and customary service. Warranty is granted against all persons in perpetuity. Sealed in witness.
Hiis testibus: Willelmo de Thelnitham, Johanne filio Willelmi de Berdewell, Radulfo de Berdewell, et aliis.

Ixworth Thorpe, Sunday 23 Sept. 1291

117. Grant in heredity by John de Verdun (*Werdon'*) to William brother of John of Pakenham, kt, for his service and ten marks sterling in cash, of a messuage with croft, buildings, ditches and trees in the vill of Ixworth Thorpe beside the messuage and croft of Nicholas Schanke, and of two acres of arable land in the vill of Honington (*Honegton'*) with all appurtenances in the field called

Clakysmedwe beside the land of the church of Honington, to hold and to have of the grantor and his heirs by William and his heirs or whosoever to whom he may wish to grant, sell, or in anyway assign it, freely, quit, well, peaceably and by inheritance, rendering each year to the capital lord of the fee the due and customary service and to the grantor and his heirs a clove at Michaelmas for all services, aids, and customs. Warranty is granted against all persons. Sealed in witness.
Hiis testibus: Petro de Thelnitham, Willelmo de eadem, Radulfo de Berdewell, Johanne filio Willelmi, Roberto ultra aquam, Willelmo de Willyngham, Petro de Thorp', et aliis.

[Late thirteenth century, before 1290]

118. Grant in heredity by Thomas the chaplain of Bardwell (*Berdewell*) to Thomas son of William of Pakenham, kt, and Alice his wife, for a certain sum of money in cash, of a piece of arable land lying in the field of Ixworth Thorpe between the land of Thomas on the one side and that of Walter Kenne on the other, abutting at one headland on the road that leads from the church of Ixworth Thorpe to Bardwell,[a] to have and to hold of the capital lord of the fee by Thomas, Alice and Thomas's heirs or assigns by the due and customary service. Warranty is granted against all persons in perpetuity. Sealed in witness.
Hiis testibus: Ricardo de Wykes, Johanne de Berdewell', Petro de Thelnitham, Waltero Kenne, Willelmo le Warde, et aliis.

Bardwell, 12 March 1309

a 'Sapiston' underlined in cancellation.

119. [*fo. 17v*] Acknowledgement by William Toffay of Ixworth Thorpe that he is bound to the payment to Thomas son of *dominus* William of Pakenham, kt, and his heirs or assigns, for his messuage and three acres of arable land with appurtenances in the vills of Ixworth Thorpe, Honington (*Honeton'*), and Troston, of 2d of rent paid annually at Michaelmas to Thomas and his heirs or assigns or to whomever might acquire the messuage and three acres of land in perpetuity. Sealed in witness.
Hiis testibus: Johanne de Berdewell, Ricardo de Wykes, Petro de Thelnitham, Waltero Kenne, Roberto Atehil, et aliis.

Ixworth Thorpe, Thursday 10 April 1309

120. Grant in heredity by William le Warde of Ixworth Thorpe to Thomas son of *dominus* William of Pakenham, kt, and Alice his wife, for a certain sum of money in cash, of the homage and service of Robert son of Ralph of Ixworth Thorpe with 6d of annual rents, to have and to hold by Thomas, Alice, and Thomas's heirs or assigns of the capital lords of the fees by the due and customary service. Warranty is granted for the foresaid 7d (*sic*) of annual rents against all persons in perpetuity. Sealed in witness.

Hiis testibus: Petro de Thelnitham, Henrico de Berdewell, Waltero Kenne, Johanne de Suthenton', Roberto Atehil', et aliis.

Ixworth Thorpe, Sunday 9 March 1309

121. Grant in heredity by Walter le Syre, chaplain, to *dominus* William of Pakenham, kt, for his service and 2s sterling in cash, of 2d of annual rents, that is, 1d from Robert Dispenser (*le Spenser*) for a tenement that he held from the grantor at *Longefurlong*, and 1d from Walter le Bor for a tenement that he held from the grantor at *Longefurlong*, with homages, wardships, reliefs, escheats and all other things that pertain to the said rents, to hold and to have of the grantor and his heirs by William and his heirs or assigns, freely, quit, well, peaceably and by inheritance, rendering therefrom annually each year to the grantor and his heirs a clove at Easter for all services, aids and demands. Warranty is granted against all persons in perpetuity. Sealed in witness.
Hiis testibus: Willelmo de Thelnitham, Radulfo de Berdewell, Johanne filio Willelmi, Roberto ultra aquam, Ricardo de Suthenton', Ricardo de Bernham, et aliis.

[Third quarter of thirteenth century, before 1283]

122. Grant in heredity by William of Willingham (*Wilingham*) to *dominus* William of Pakenham, kt, for his service and 20s sterling in cash, of an acre of arable land in the vill of Ixworth Thorpe between the land of *dominus* William and that of John Hereward, abutting at one headland on *le Bek* and the other on the land of Walter Widre, be there more or less, to hold and to have of the grantor and his heirs by *dominus* William and his heirs, freely, quit, well, peaceably, in fee and heredity, [*fo. 18r*] rendering therefrom annually to the grantor and his heirs a clove at Michaelmas for all services, aids, all manner of suit of court and secular demands. Warranty is granted against all persons in perpetuity. Sealed in witness.
Hiis testibus: Radulfo de Berdewell, Johanne filio Willelmi, Ricardo de Suthenton', Willelmo le Warde, Petro de Thorp', et aliis.

[Third quarter of thirteenth century, before 1283]

123. Grant in heredity by Richard of Barnham (*Bernham*) to *dominus* William of Pakenham, kt, for his service and 10s sterling in cash, of three roods of arable land in the vill of Ixworth Thorpe in the field called *le Bromlond*, of which two roods lie beside the land of the church of Ixworth Thorpe, abutting at one headland on *le Melleneweye*, and one rood beside the land of William, abutting at one headland on the foresaid road, be there more or less, to hold and to have of the grantor and his heirs by William and his heirs or whosoever to whom he may wish to grant, sell or assign it, freely, quit, well, peaceably and in heredity, rendering therefrom annually to the grantor and his heirs a clove at Easter for all services, aids, all manner of suit of court and demands. Warranty is granted against all persons in perpetuity. Sealed in witness.

Hiis testibus: Willelmo de Thelnitham, Radulfo de Berdewell, Johanne filio Willelmi, Roberto ultra aquam, Johanne le Syre, Petro de Thorp', et aliis.

[Late thirteenth century, before 1290]

124. Grant in heredity by John of Thorpe (*Thorp'*), smith (*faber*), to *dominus* William of Pakenham, kt, of one acre and one rood of arable land in Ixworth Thorpe in the field called *Northolm* between the lands of William on both sides, abutting at one headland on the common pasture[a] of Ixworth Thorpe, be there more or less, to have and to hold by William and his heirs and his assigns of the capital lord of the fee, freely, quit, well, peaceably and in heredity, rendering therefrom annually to the same capital lord the due and customary service for all services, aids, customs and demands. Warranty is granted against all persons in perpetuity. Sealed in witness.
Hiis testibus: Radulfo de Berdewell, Johanne filio Willelmi, Willelmo de Thelnitham, Petro filio suo, Bartholomeo de Lyvermere, Symone de Gesselingham, et aliis.

[1290 x 1300]

a 'terram' underlined in cancellation.

125. Grant in heredity by Peter of Elmswell (*Elimswell'*), son of Walter de Herst, to *dominus* William of Pakenham, kt, and Thomas and William his sons, of three acres of land in Ixworth Thorpe, of which two acres lie in the field called *Toftys* beside the land of William, abutting on the land of the prior and convent of Ixworth towards the east, and one acre lies in the same field between the land of Walter Widre on one side and the land which was formerly of Walter the chaplain on the other, be there more or less, to have and to hold of the capital lords of the fees by *dominus* William, Thomas, William and the heirs of Thomas and William or their assigns, freely, quit and honourably and in heredity, rendering therefrom to the said capital lords the due and customary service for all services, customs, and secular demands. Warranty is granted [*fo. 18v*] against all persons in perpetuity. Sealed in witness.
Hiis testibus: Radulfo de Berdewell, Johanne filio Willelmi, Roberto ultra aquam, Petro de Thorp', Symone de Gesselingham, Thoma Revel, et aliis.

[1290 x 1300]

126. Grant in heredity by Cecily of Brakelond and Thomas the chaplain, her son, to *dominus* William of Pakenham, kt, and the lady Johanna his wife, of three roods of arable land in Ixworth Thorpe lying in the field called *le Tuftis* between the lands of William on both sides, be there more or less, to hold and to have by William, Johanna and William's heirs of the capital lord of the fee by the due and customary service, freely, quit, peaceably and in heredity, for all services and secular demands. Warranty is granted against all persons. Sealed in witness with their seals.

Hiis testibus: Radulfo de Berdewell, Johanne filio Willelmi de eadem, Roberto de Drenkyston', et aliis.

[1290 x 1300]

127. Grant in heredity by John Bonihard and Johanna his wife to *dominus* William of Pakenham, kt, of an acre of arable land in Ixworth Thorpe at *Tuftes* between the lands of William on both sides, abutting at each headland on the land of William, be there more or less, to hold and to have by William and his heirs and assigns of the capital lord of the fee by the due and customary service, freely, well, in peace, in fee and heredity, for all services, customs and demands. Warranty is granted against all persons in perpetuity. Sealed in witness.
Hiis testibus: Radulfo de Berdewell, Johanne filio Willelmi de eadem, Willelmo de Thelnitham, Petro de Thorp', et aliis.

[1290 x 1300]

128. Grant in heredity by John Louwyn of Ixworth Thorpe to *dominus* William of Pakenham, kt, of two and a half acres of land in Ixworth Thorpe in *Coliscroft* between the lands of William on both sides, be there more or less, to hold and to have by William and his heirs and assigns, freely, quit, in fee and heredity in perpetuity. Warranty is granted against all persons in perpetuity. Sealed in witness.
Hiis testibus: Symone de Gesselingham, Willelmo le Warde, Roberto filio Radulfi, Roberto de Drenkyston', Thoma Revel, Petro de Thorp', et aliis.

[Late thirteenth century, before 1290]

129. Grant in heredity by William of Willingham (*Wilingham*) of Troston to *dominus* William of Pakenham, for 20s sterling which he gave to him, of an acre of arable land in Ixworth Thorpe beside the land of William Burchard, abutting at one headland on the land of the prior of Ixworth (*Ixeworth'*), be there more or less, to have and to hold of the capital lords of the fees by *dominus* William, his heirs or assigns, freely, quit, well, peaceably, in fee and heredity by the due and customary service. Warranty is granted against all persons in perpetuity. Sealed in witness.
Hiis testibus: domino Reginaldo Peche, milite, Willelmo de Thelnitham, [*fo. 19r*] Radulfo de Berdewell, Roberto ultra aquam, Symone de Gesselingham, Roberto filio Radulfi, Petro de Thorp', et aliis.

[1290 x 1300]

130. Grant in heredity by Geoffrey son of John the marshal (*le marchelchal*) of Troston (*Stroston'*) to *dominus* William of Pakenham, for his service and 3s of silver in cash, of 3d of annual rents, that is, 1d from Robert le Dispenser for a tenement that he held of the grantor at *Surswell'*, and 2d from Robert Puttok for a tenement that he held of the grantor beside his messuage, with homages, reliefs, wardships, assarts and with all other things which might accrue to the grantor

from the said rents, to hold and to have of the grantor and his heirs by *dominus* William and his heirs or assigns, freely, quit, well, peaceably and in heredity, rendering therefrom each year to the grantor and his heirs a clove at Easter for all services, aids, all manner of suit of court and secular demands. Warranty is granted against all persons in perpetuity. Sealed in witness.
Hiis testibus: Willelmo de Thelnitham, Radulfo de Berdewell, Roberto ultra aquam, Radulfo filio Symonis, Willelmo de Wilingham, et aliis.
[Late thirteenth century, before 1290]

131. Mandate by Edmund of Pakenham, kt, to all free tenants and others of the manor of Ixworth Thorpe. Since he enfeoffed Thomas his brother with the manor of Ixworth Thorpe with appurtenances without any reservation, except the fishery which *dominus* William his father formerly acquired from William de Criketot, kt, he requests and commands that that they submit and answer to Thomas according to the form of the charter of enfeoffment which he made to him for the manor. Sealed in witness.

Norton, 7 Nov. 1304

132. Quitclaim by Thomas son of Margaret le Veisse de Brunham for himself and his heirs to Thomas of Pakenham, son of *dominus* William, kt, and his heirs and his assigns, of all right which he has and claim which he had or in anyway might have from the inheritance of a certain Ralph Grunam in the vills of Ixworth Thorpe and Honington (*Huneton'*), so that neither Thomas nor his heirs nor anyone in their name may henceforth in perpetuity have any right or claim in the said two vills by inheritance. Sealed in witness.
Hiis testibus: Waltero Kenne, Roberto filio Radulfi de Thorp' Ixeworth, et aliis.

Ixworth Thorpe, Sunday 9 Feb. 1309

133. Notification by William of Pakenham, kt, that he has given power of attorney to his most beloved Alexander of Stanton to take, in the grantor's name, full seisin of a certain piece of land, with appurtenances, which the grantor purchased from John Louwyn of Ixworth Thorpe in *Colistoft*, as is contained more fully in John's charter which enfeoffed the grantor. Sealed in witness as letters patent.

Norton, Wednesday 3 Nov. 1294

134. [*fo. 19v*] Grant in heredity by Thomas the chaplain of Ixworth Thorpe to Thomas of Pakenham and Alice his wife, for a certain sum of money in cash, of a rood of meadow with appurtenances, being fit to be mowed (*falcabilis*), lying in the meadow of Ixworth Thorpe called *le Gorehil'* between the meadow of Thomas on both sides, of which one headland abuts on the river bank leading from Ixworth (*Ixeworth*) towards Bardwell (*Berdewell*), be there more or less, to have and to hold by Thomas, Alice and Thomas's heirs of the capital lord of the

fee by the due and customary service. Warranty is granted against all persons in perpetuity. Sealed in witness.
Hiis testibus: Waltero Kenne, Roberto de le Hil', et aliis.

Ixworth Thorpe (*Thorp'*), Saturday 27 Feb. 1311

135. Quitclaim by Geoffrey son of Geoffrey of Thorpe (*Thorp' Ixeworth'*) to Thomas of Pakenham and his heirs or assigns of all right which he has and claim which he had or in anyway might have in all that land which he had from the grant and demise of the late Geoffrey, his father, in the foresaid vill of Ixworth Thorpe, for which land he himself pleaded in the court of the lord king by writ, to have and to hold by the grantee and his heirs in perpetuity, so that neither Geoffrey nor his heirs nor his assigns nor anyone for them nor in their name may henceforth have any right or claim or part in the whole land in perpetuity. Sealed in witness.
Hiis testibus: Johanne de Berdewell, Petro de Thelnitham, Henrico de Thurston', Roberto filio Radulfi, Waltero Kenne, et aliis.

[After 1305, perhaps 1309]

136. Grant in heredity by Robert son of Ralph of Ixworth Thorpe to Thomas son of *dominus* William of Pakenham, kt, and Alice his wife, for a certain sum of money in cash, of a piece of arable land with a herbage lying by it, which, with its appurtenances, lies at Broadwater (*Bradwater*) between the lands of Thomas on both sides, abutting at one headland on the land of Thomas and the other on the meadow of William le Warde, to have and to hold by Thomas, Alice and Thomas's heirs or assigns of the capital lord of the fee by the due and customary service. Warranty is granted against all persons in perpetuity. Sealed in witness.
Hiis testibus: Johanne de Berdewell', Henrico de Berdewell', Petro de Thelnitham, Waltero Kenne, Roberto de le Hil', et aliis.

Ixworth Thorpe (*Thorp' Ixeworth'*), 1 May 1309

137. Grant in heredity by William le Warde of Ixworth Thorpe to Thomas of Pakenham and Alice his wife, for a certain sum of money in cash, of three roods of meadow fit to be mowed (*falcabilis*) with appurtenances lying in the meadow of Ixworth Thorpe called *le Gorehil* between the meadow of Thomas on one side and that of Robert son of Ralph on the other, of which one headland abuts on the herbage of Thomas, be there more or less, to have and to hold by Thomas, Alice, and Thomas's heirs of the capital lord of the fee by the due and customary service. [*fo. 20r*] Warranty is granted against all persons in perpetuity. Sealed in witness.
Hiis testibus: Waltero Kenne, Roberto filio Radulfi, Galfrido fratre suo, Thoma Hog', Johanne Louwyne, et aliis.

Ixworth Thorpe (*Thorp'*), Thursday 23 July 1310

138. Grant in heredity by Philip the farrier (*le ferour*) of Ixworth Thorpe to Thomas of Pakenham and Alice his wife, for a certain sum of money in cash, of a quarter of a rood of meadow fit to be mowed (*falcabilis*) with appurtenances lying in the meadow of Ixworth Thorpe called *Gorehil'* between the meadow of William le Warde on both sides, of which one headland abuts on the meadow of William, be there more or less, to have and to hold by Thomas, Alice, and Thomas's heirs of the capital lord of the fee by the due and customary service. Warranty is granted against all persons in perpetuity. Sealed in witness.
Hiis testibus: Waltero Kenne, Roberto filio Radulfi, Galfrido fratre suo, Thoma Hog', Johanne Louwyn, et aliis.

Ixworth Thorpe (*Thorp'*), Thursday 16 July 1310

139. Grant in heredity by Benedict le Bor of Ixworth Thorpe to Thomas of Pakenham and Alice his wife, for a certain sum of money in cash, of one and a half acres of arable land with appurtenances lying in the field of Ixworth Thorpe, of which one acre lies on *le Breche* between the lands of William le Warde and the prior of Ixworth (*Ixeworth'*), of which one headland abuts on the land of John le Syre, and half an acre lies at *Wetelundys* beside the land of Thomas, of which one headland abuts on *le Greneweye*, to have and to hold by Thomas, Alice, and Thomas's heirs of the capital lord of the fee by the due and customary service. Warranty is granted against all persons in perpetuity. Sealed in witness.
Hiis testibus: Waltero Kenne, Roberto filio Radulfi, Galfrido fratre suo, Thoma Hog', et aliis.

Ixworth Thorpe (*Thorp'*), 23 Nov. 1307

140. Grant in heredity by John le Syre the younger of Ixworth Thorpe to Thomas of Pakenham and Alice his wife, for a certain sum of money which they gave to him, of a half acre and ten perches of arable land with appurtenances with eight perches of herbage with appurtenances together lying in the field of Ixworth Thorpe called Broadwater (*Bradwater*) beside the land of Thomas, of which one headland abuts on the land of Thomas called *Surswell'*, to have and to hold by Thomas, Alice, and Thomas's heirs of the capital lord of the fee by the due and customary service. Warranty is granted against all persons in perpetuity. Sealed in witness.
Hiis testibus: Waltero Kenne, Roberto filio Radulfi, Galfrido fratre suo, Willelmo le Warde, Thoma Hog', et aliis.

Ixworth Thorpe (*Thorp'*), 4 April 1310

141. [*fo. 20v*] Quitclaim by William son of Robert Knight (*le Knyght*) of Pakenham for himself and his heirs or assigns to Thomas of Pakenham and Alice his wife and Thomas's heirs or assigns of all right which he has and claim which he had or in anyway might have in a piece of meadow fit to be mowed (*falcabilis*) with appurtenances lying in the vill of Ixworth Thorpe at *Brodynge* between the meadow of Thomas on both sides, of which one headland lies on the common river bank, namely, that foresaid piece of meadow which Thomas and Alice

acquired by a grant from Alice the grantor's mother, to have and to hold by Thomas, Alice, and Thomas's heirs or assigns, so that neither William nor his heirs nor anyone in their name may henceforth have any right or claim in the piece of meadow against Thomas, Alice, or Thomas's heirs and assigns. Sealed in witness.
Hiis testibus: Ricardo de Wykes, Johanne de Berdewell', Waltero Kenne de Thorp', Roberto de le Hil', et aliis.

Ixworth Thorpe (*Thorp'*), Wednesday 12 May 1311

142. Quitclaim by Richard Armerard of Bardwell (*Berdewell*) for himself and his heirs in perpetuity to Robert Knight (*le Knyght*) de Galthowe and his heirs or assigns for a certain sum of money in cash, of all right which he has and claim which he had or in anyway might have or which in anyway might fall due or accrue in half an acre of meadow lying in Ixworth Thorpe beside the river bank running from Ixworth (*Ixeworth'*) towards Bardwell (*Berdewell'*), abutting at one headland on the meadow of *dominus* William of Pakenham, be there more or less, so that henceforth neither Richard nor his heirs nor any one for him nor in the name of his heirs may have any right or claim in the half acre of meadow or against Robert Knight, his heirs or assigns in perpetuity. Sealed in witness.
Hiis testibus: Roberto filio Radulfi, Galfrido fratre suo, Waltero Kenne, Johanne Louwyne, et aliis.

Pakenham, Saturday 11 June 1300

143. Grant in heredity by Alice widow of Robert Knight (*le Knyght*) of Pakenham to Thomas of Pakenham and Alice his wife, for a certain sum of money in cash, of a piece of meadow fit to be mowed (*falcabilis*) with appurtenances lying in the vill of Ixworth Thorpe at *Brodyng* between the meadow of Thomas on both sides, abutting at one headland on the river bank leading from Ixworth (*Ixeworth'*) to Bardwell (*Berdewell'*), to have [and to hold] by Thomas, Alice, and Thomas's heirs of the capital lord of the fee by the due and customary service. Warranty is granted against all persons in perpetuity. Sealed in witness.
Hiis testibus: Ricardo de Wykes, Johanne de Berdewell', Waltero Kenne de Thorp', Roberto filio Radulfi, Roberto de le Hil' de Berdewell', et aliis.

Ixworth Thorpe (*Thorp'*), Wednesday 12 May 1311

144. [*fo. 25r*] Quitclaim by Adam Armerard of Bardwell (*Berdewell'*) for himself and his heirs or his assigns to Thomas of Pakenham, Alice his wife and Thomas's heirs, of all right which he has and claim which he had or in anyway might have by any title or which might come to him and his heirs through inheritance after the death of William Armerard his father in a piece of meadow fit to be mowed (*falcabilis*) with appurtenances in the vill of Ixworth Thorpe at *Brodynge* between the meadow of Thomas on both sides, abutting at one headland on the common river bank, which Thomas and Alice have from the grant of Alice the quitclaimer's sister, to have and to hold by Thomas, Alice, and Thomas's heirs or assigns, so that neither Adam nor his heirs or anyone in his

name may henceforth have any right or claim in the piece of meadow with appurtenances in perpetuity. Sealed in witness.
Hiis testibus: Ricardo de Wykes, Johanne de Berdewell', Waltero Kenne de Thorp', Radulfo filio Radulfi, Roberto de le Hil de Berdewell', et aliis.

Ixworth Thorpe, Wednesday 12 May 1311

145. Grant in heredity by Robert son of Ralph of Ixworth Thorpe to Thomas of Pakenham and Alice his wife, for a certain sum of money in cash, of two acres and six perches of meadow lying in the meadow of Ixworth Thorpe called *le Gorehil'* beside the meadow of William Neweman, abutting at one headland on the river bank running from Ixworth (*Ixeworth'*) to Bardwell (*Berdewell'*), to have and to hold by Thomas, Alice, and Thomas's heirs or assigns of the capital lord of the fee by the due and customary service. Warranty is granted against all persons in perpetuity. Sealed in witness.
Hiis testibus: Willelmo le Syre, Waltero Kenne, Nicholao le Syre, Willelmo le Warde, Willelmo Louwyn, et aliis.

Ixworth Thorpe, Sunday 2 Aug. 1310

146. Quitclaim in perpetuity by William le Syre of Ixworth Thorpe for himself and his heirs or assigns to Robert son of Ralph of Ixworth Thorpe and his heirs or assigns, of all right which he has and claim that he has, had, or in anyway might have in a piece of meadow lying in the meadow of Ixworth Thorpe called *le Gorehil'*, as testified by the charter of enfeoffment which he had from Robert, to have and to hold through the grantor and his heirs or assigns of the capital lord of the fee by the due and customary service, and paying therefrom annually to Robert and his heirs or assigns 40s of silver at Michaelmas for the meadow, which has been reckoned to be two acres and six perches. Sealed in witness.
Hiis testibus: Waltero Kenne, Willelmo le Warde, Johanne Louwyne, Roberto de le Hil', et aliis.

Ixworth Thorpe, Monday 27 July 1310

147. Grant in heredity by William of Hinderclay (*Hindircle*) to Thomas of Pakenham [*fo. 25v*] and Alice his wife, of a messuage with appurtenances lying in the vill of Ixworth Thorpe between the messuage of Thomas on one side and that of the grantor on the other, abutting at one headland on the common pasture of Ixworth Thorpe and at the other on the land of Thomas, to have and to hold the messuage with appurtenances of the capital lords of the fees by the due and customary service by Thomas, Alice, and Thomas's heirs or by whoever to whom Thomas, after the death of Alice his wife, may legally grant, sell or assign it, freely, quit, in fee and heredity. Warranty is granted against all persons in perpetuity. Sealed in witness.
Hiis testibus: Johanne de Berdewell', Petro de Thelnitham, Waltero Kenne, Willelmo filio eius, Roberto filio Radulfi, et aliis.

Ixworth Thorpe, Thursday 6 March 1309

148. Agreement between Thomas of Pakenham on the one hand and William Kenne of Ixworth Thorpe on the other, whereby Thomas granted to William one rood and six perches of pasture lying on the edge of the meadow of Ixworth Thorpe called *le Hildyng* between the land of Nicholas le Syre on the one side and the meadow of Thomas le Ferour, chaplain, on the other, of which one headland abuts on the pasture of Robert Hereward, and six perches of pasture lie at *Sutholm* between the pastures of William of Pakenham and Thomas Hog, of which one headland lies on the land of Thomas of Pakenham, be there more or less, to have and to hold by William and his heirs of the capital lord of the fee by the due and customary service; and William granted to Thomas one rood and two and a half perches of pasture lying on the edge of the meadow of Ixworth Thorpe called *Banegrave*, that is, in all places where ever William had pasture from *Thorpehalleyerd* up to the bridge of John of Bardwell (*Berdewell'*) between the arable lands and meadows fit to be mowed (*falcabilis*), to have and to hold by Thomas and his heirs of the capital lord of the fee by the due and customary service. Warranty is granted against all persons in perpetuity. Sealed respectively by each party.
Hiis testibus: Johanne de Berdewello, Johanne de Suthenton', Roberto filio Radulfi de Thorp', Willelmo le Warde et aliis.

Ixworth Thorpe, Saturday 13 May 1312

149. Quitclaim by William le Warde of Ixworth Thorpe for himself and his heirs to Thomas son of *dominus* William of Pakenham, kt, and his heirs, of all right which he has and claim which he had or in anyway might have in two pieces[a] of arable land with appurtenances lying in *Schortebreche*, and also of all form of remission and action which he might have against Thomas, so that neither William nor his heirs nor anyone in their name might henceforth have any right or claim in the land in perpetuity. Sealed in witness.
Hiis testibus: Waltero Kenne, Roberto filio Radulfi, Nicholao le Syre, Johanne Louwyn, Roberto de le Hil de Berdewell', et aliis.

Tuesday 21 Nov. 1307

a 'acris' underlined for cancellation.

150. [*fo. 26r*] Grant in heredity by William son of John le Syre the elder of Ixworth Thorpe to Thomas of Pakenham and Alice his wife, for a certain sum of money in cash, of half an acre and ten perches of arable land with appurtenances together with eight perches of herbage lying in the field of Ixworth Thorpe called Broadwater (*Bradwater*) beside the land of Thomas, of which one headland abuts on the land of Thomas, to have and to hold by Thomas, Alice, and Thomas's heirs of the capital lord of the fee by the due and customary service. Warranty is granted against all persons in perpetuity. Sealed in witness.
Hiis testibus: Waltero Kenne, Roberto filio Radulfi, Galfrido fratre suo, Willelmo le Warde, Thoma Hog, et aliis.

Ixworth Thorpe, 4 April 1310

151. Grant in heredity by William le Warde of Ixworth Thorpe to Thomas of Pakenham and Alice his wife, for a certain sum of money in cash, of one and a half roods and seven perches of meadow fit to be mowed (*falcabilis*) with appurtenances lying in the meadow of Ixworth Thorpe called *le Gorehil* below one piece of meadow, that is, around one headland to the other headland between the meadow of Thomas and the river bank, of which one headland abuts on the river bank, to have and to hold by Thomas, Alice, and Thomas's heirs of the capital lord of the fee by the due and customary service. Warranty is granted against all persons in perpetuity. Sealed in witness.
Hiis testibus: Waltero Kenne, Roberto filio Radulfi, Galfrido fratre suo, Thoma Hog, et aliis.

Ixworth Thorpe (*Thorp'*), Friday 17 July 1310

152. Agreement between Thomas of Pakenham on the one hand and William le Syre of Ixworth Thorpe on the other, whereby William granted to Thomas, for a certain sum of money in cash, a piece of land lying in the field of Ixworth Thorpe called *Schamelocys* beside the land of Thomas, of which one headland abuts on the road leading from the wood of John of Bardwell (*Berdewell'*) to the church of Ixworth Thorpe; and half an acre with appurtenances lying in the same field called *Redakr* beside the land of Thomas, abutting at one headland on the land of Thomas; and one piece of herbage lying at *Brodyng* beside the herbage of Thomas, abutting at one headland on the meadow of Walter Kenne. In exchange, Thomas granted to William one piece of land lying in the field of Ixworth Thorpe beside the messuage and land of William, abutting at one headland on the messuage of William; and half an acre of land lying in the same field beside the land of Thomas, abutting at one headland on the messuage of William; and one piece of herbage lying at one headland of the said piece of land beside the herbage of William; [*fo. 26v*] to have and to hold by Thomas and his heirs or assigns and by William and his heirs or assigns of the capital lords of the fees by the due and customary service. Warranty is granted against all persons in perpetuity. Sealed respectively by both parties.
Hiis testibus: Petro de Thelnitham, Waltero Kenne, Roberto filio Radulfi, Nicholao le Syre, Johanne Louwyn, et aliis.

Ixworth Thorpe, Monday 27 July 1310

153. Agreement whereby Thomas son of *dominus* William of Pakenham, kt, granted in exchange to Robert son of Ralph of Ixworth Thorpe five acres of arable land and three roods with appurtenances in Ixworth Thorpe, of which four acres and a rood with appurtenances lie in the field called *Leyerescroft* between the land of Robert on the one side and that of Thomas on the other, abutting at one headland on *Borelishalwaker*, and one acre and twelve perches with appurtenances lie in the field called *le Toftys* between the land of Thomas on the one side and that of Robert on the other, abutting at one headland on the land of Robert, and half an acre with appurtenances which is called *le Borelshalakyr* lying in the same field between the land of Robert on both sides, abutting at one headland on the land of Robert, to have and to hold by him and his heirs of the capital lords of

the fees by the due and customary service; and Robert gave in exchange to Thomas five and a half acres of land with appurtenances in Ixworth Thorpe, of which two acres of land and three roods lie beside *Gorehille* between the land of Thomas on both sides, abutting at one headland on the land of Geoffrey son of Ralph of Ixworth Thorpe, and two acres of land and three roods of land with appurtenances lie in the field called *le Wetelondys* between the lands of Thomas lying around it, abutting at one headland on *le Chercheweye*, to have and to hold by him and his heirs of the capital lords of the fees by the due and customary service. Warranty is granted in perpetuity. Sealed respectively by both parties.
Hiis testibus: Ricardo de Wykes, Petro de Thelnitham, Johanne de Berdewell', Henrico de eadem, Johanne de Suthenton', et aliis.

Ixworth Thorpe, Tuesday 19 March 1308

154. Agreement between Thomas of Pakenham on the one side and Thomas Hog of Ixworth Thorpe on the other, whereby the foresaid Thomas granted to Thomas Hoc two acres and one rood of arable land with appurtenances lying by the church of Ixworth Thorpe between the lands of Thomas of Pakenham and William le Syre, abutting at one headland on the king's highway, to have and to hold by Thomas Hog and his heirs of the capital lord of the fee by the due and customary service, namely, 1d at Michaelmas; and Thomas Hog granted to Thomas of Pakenham two acres and one rood of arable land with appurtenances lying in the field of Ixworth Thorpe, of which one acre and half a rood of land with appurtenances lie at *Schamelocys* between the lands of Thomas of Pakenham on both sides, abutting at one headland on the land of Thomas of Pakenham, and one acre and half a rood with appurtenances lie at Broadwater (*Bradewater*) between the lands of Thomas of Pakenham on both sides, abutting at one headland on the land of Thomas of Pakenham, to have and [*fo. 27r*] to hold by Thomas of Pakenham and his heirs of the capital lord of the fee by the due and customary service. Warranty is granted against all persons in perpetuity. Sealed respectively by both parties.
Hiis testibus: Waltero Kenne, Willelmo filio suo, Roberto filio Radulfi, Galfrido fratre suo, et aliis.

Ixworth Thorpe, 25 Jan. 1312

155. Exchange whereby Edmund Dispenser (*Dispensator*) of Bardwell (*Berdewell'*) granted in exchange to Thomas of Pakenham son of *dominus* William of Pakenham, kt, an acre of meadow in the part of Ixworth Thorpe called *Brodyng* between the meadow of Thomas and that of John son of William, abutting at one headland on the river bank running from Ixworth Thorpe to Bardwell (*Berdewell'*), in return for an acre and four perches of meadow lying in the said meadow between the meadow of the grantor and that of Thomas, abutting at one headland on the foresaid river bank, to have and to hold of the capital lords of the fees by the due and customary service, freely, quit, well, in peace, in fee and heredity. Warranty is granted against all persons in perpetuity. Sealed in witness.
Hiis testibus: Johanne filio Willelmi, Henrico de Berdewell', Johanne de

Suthenton', Roberto de le Hil, Roberto Precuis, Waltero Kenne, Willelmo filio suo, Roberto filio Radulfi, Johanne Louwyn de Thorpe', et aliis.

Ixworth Thorpe, 25 July 1310

156. Acknowledgement by Walter Kenne of Ixworth Thorpe that he is obligated to Thomas of Pakenham in a certain annual rent of 4d payable to Thomas and his heirs and assigns in perpetuity, that is, at Michaelmas 2d and at Easter 2d, for five roods of land, or more if there be so, lying in the field of Ixworth Thorpe between the land of Thomas on both sides, abutting at one headland on *Wellegate Weye* and the other on *le Chercheweye*, so that it is lawful for Thomas to distrain upon the land for the rent should it fall into arrears, whether in part or in whole. Sealed in witness.
Hiis testibus: Matheo de Thelnitham, Johanne de Berdewell', Petro de Redligworth, Bartholomo de Lyvermere, Roberto filio Radulfi de Thorp', et aliis.

Ixworth Thorpe, 24 Aug. 1310

157. Grant in heredity by William le Warde of Ixworth Thorpe to Thomas of Pakenham of a piece of his meadow fit to be mowed (*falcabilis*) lying in *Sutholm* between the meadow of Thomas on both sides, abutting at one headland on the meadow of Thomas, be there more or less, to have and to hold of the capital lord of the fee by [*fo. 27v*] Thomas and his heirs or assigns by the due and customary service. Warranty is granted against all persons in perpetuity. Sealed in witness.
Hiis testibus: Waltero Kenne, Willelmo Kenne, Roberti filio Radulfi, Johanne Louwyn, et aliis.

Ixworth Thorpe, 3 March 1311

158. Agreement between Thomas son William of Pakenham, kt, on the one hand and Walter Kenne of Ixworth Thorpe and William his son on the other, whereby Thomas granted in exchange to Walter and William seven acres of land lying in the field of Honington (*Huneton'*), of which two acres lie in the quarter which is called *Passewong* beside the land of John of Bardwell (*Berdewell'*), abutting at one headland on the common pasture of Honington; and two acres lie beside the land of Matilda le Smeth of Honington, abutting at one headland on *Blodhowepathton'*; and two and a half acres lie in the said field situated in the quarter which is called *Passewong*, abutting on the herbage of John le Man; and three roods lie on *le Ronakerhil'* beside the land of John le Neve, abutting at one headland on *Wellegateweye*, be there more or less, to have and to hold by Walter, William, and their heirs or assigns of the capital lords of the fees in perpetuity, freely, quit, well, peaceably by the due and customary service. Walter and William granted in exchange to Thomas seven acres of land lying in the field of Ixworth Thorpe, of which four and a half acres lie in *le Bronstlede* between the land of Thomas of Pakenham on both sides, abutting at one headland on the herbage of Thomas; and half an acre lies between the land of Thomas lying around it; and two acres of land lie at *Churchswell'* between the land of Thomas

on both sides, to have and to hold by Thomas and his heirs or assigns with all their appurtenances of the capital lords of the fees in perpetuity, freely, well, peaceably by the due and customary service. Warranty is granted by both parties in perpetuity. Sealed respectively by both parties.
Hiis testibus: Matheo de Thelnitham, Johanne de Berdewell', Petro de Thelnitham, Petro de Redligworth', Bartholomeo de Lyvermere, Roberto filio Radulfi de Thorp Ixeworth[a], et aliis.

Ixworth Thorpe (*Thorp' Ixeworth'*), Sunday 23 Aug. 1310

a 'Ixworth' is supplied by the original, BL Harleian Charter 54 F 1. Single-sheet original, bottom portion of a chirograph, approx. 230mm wide x 175mm; seal 1, round, approx. 25mm, natural wax, illegible; seal 2, round, approx. 30mm, natural wax, eight-pointed star, illegible.

159. Quitclaim by Walter Kenne of Ixworth Thorpe (*Thorp'*), Robert son of Ralph of the same, Geoffrey son of Ralph of the same, John Louwyn of the same, John le Syre the younger of the same, Nicholas son of Robert le Syre of the same for themselves and their heirs or assigns to Thomas son of William of Pakenham, kt, and his heirs or assigns, of all right and claim which they had or in anyway might have or which in anyway might fall due or accrue by any titular right in the heath called *Spynheth* in the vill of Ixworth Thorpe, so that neither Walter, Robert, Geoffrey, John, John, Nicholas, nor their heirs nor anyone in their name may henceforth have any right or claim in the heath in perpetuity. Sealed in witness by all the quitclaimers.
Hiis testibus: Ricardo de Wykes, Henrico de Berdewell', Johanne de Suthenton', Petro de [*fo. 28r*] Thelnitham, Roberto de le Hil' de Berdewell', et aliis.

Ixworth Thorpe, Saturday 8 July 1307

160. Quitclaim by Walter Kenne of Ixworth Thorpe, Robert son of Ralph of the same, Geoffrey his brother, John Louwyn, John le Syre the elder, John le Syre the younger, Nicholas le Syre, William Warde, Thomas Hog, Stephen Hog for themselves and their heirs to Thomas of Pakenham and his heirs of the road lying beside the messuage of Thomas Hog and lying in the same quarter and for the same length and breadth as was appointed in the exchange between Thomas and Thomas.

Ixworth Thorpe, 25 Aug. 1307

Marginal note: a certain quitclaim for the road called *Chercheweye*.

161. Quitclaim by William le Syre of Ixworth Thorpe for himself and his heirs or assigns to Thomas of Pakenham and his heirs or assigns, of all right which he has and claim which he had, has, or in anyway might have or which in anyway might fall due or accrue by any title in a piece of meadow fit to be mowed (*falcabilis*), which is reckoned at two acres and six perches, lying in the meadow of Ixworth Thorpe called *le Gorehill* beside the meadow of William Newman, abutting at one headland on the river bank running from Ixworth (*Ixeworth'*) to Bardwell

(*Berdewell*), as is testified by his charter which he has by the grant of Robert, to have and to hold by Thomas and his heirs or assigns of the capital lord of the fee by the due and customary service, so that neither William nor his heirs nor anyone in their name may henceforth have any right or claim in the foresaid two acres and six perches of meadow with appurtenances in perpetuity. Sealed in witness.
Hiis testibus: Roberto filio Radulfi, Waltero Kenne, Nicholao le Syre, et aliis.

Ixworth Thorpe, 26 May 1311

162. Grant in heredity by William le Warde of Ixworth Thorpe to Thomas of Pakenham and Alice his wife, for a certain sum of money in cash, of an acre of arable land with appurtenances lying in the field of Ixworth Thorpe called *Sutholm* beside the land of Thomas, of which one headland abuts on Broadwater (*Bradwater*) and the other on the land of John le Syre, be there more or less, to have and to hold by Thomas, Alice, and Thomas's heirs or assigns of the capital lord of the fee by the due and customary service. Warranty is granted against all persons in perpetuity. Sealed in witness.
Hiis testibus: Waltero Kenne, Willelmo filio suo, Roberto filio Radulfi, Galfrido fratre suo, Roberto de le Hil, et aliis.

Ixworth Thorpe, 1 May 1311

163. Quitclaim by William Kenne of Ixworth Thorpe for himself and his heirs to Thomas son of William of Pakenham, kt, and his heirs or assigns, of all right and claim of grazing his livestock and commoning (*pascendi cum avariis meis et communicandi*) in the vill of Ixworth Thorpe, because [*fo. 28v*] he had a certain fold, formerly of Joanlyn Feloun, in the field of Honington (*Honeweton'*), so that neither he nor his heirs nor any one in his name may henceforth have any right or claim in perpetuity. Sealed in witness.
Hiis testibus: Roberto filio Radulfi de Thorp', Galfrido fratre suo de eadem, Roberto del hil' de Berdewelle, et aliis.

Ixworth Thorpe, Sunday 7 May 1307

164. Quitclaim by Robert son of Ralph of Ixworth Thorpe for himself and his heirs or assigns to Thomas son of *dominus* William of Pakenham, kt, and his heirs or assigns, of all right which he has, which he had or in anyway might have in 2d of annual rents with all their appurtenances which came to him or might descend to his heirs, to have and to hold by Thomas and his heirs or assigns, so that neither Robert nor his heirs nor anyone in his name may henceforth have any right or claim against Thomas and his heirs or assigns in perpetuity. Sealed in witness.
Hiis testibus: Waltero Kenne, Willelmo le Warde, Nicholao le Syre, Johanne Louwyne, Roberto del hil', et aliis.

Ixworth Thorpe, 1 May 1309

165. Grant in heredity by Robert son of Ralph of Ixworth Thorpe to Thomas of Pakenham and Alice his wife, for a certain sum of money in cash, of a piece of arable land with appurtenances lying in the field of Ixworth Thorpe between the land of Robert Hereward on the one side and the road called *le Chercheweye* on the other, abutting at one headland on the drain (*exsuactum*) of Robert and the other on the tenement of Thomas, to have and to hold by Thomas and Alice until the end of their lives of the capital lords of the fees by the due and customary service, and after the deaths of Thomas and Alice, the piece of land with appurtenances shall pass to Theobald their son and Theobald's heirs in perpetuity, to hold of the capital lords of the fees by the due and customary service. Warranty is granted against all persons in perpetuity. Sealed in witness.
Hiis testibus: Willelmo de Pakynham, Thoma de Berdewell, Symone Dengyt de Thefford, Willelmo Kenne, Johanne de Southenton', Roberto del' hil, et aliis.

Ixworth Thorpe, Tuesday 6 Nov. 1313

166. [*fo. 29r*] Grant in heredity by Robert son of Ralph of Ixworth Thorpe to William son of William le Syre of Ixworth Thorpe of the homage and service of Walter Kenne with all the money from annual rents; and the homage and service of John le Syre the elder with 5d of annual rents; and the homage and service of Nicholas le Syre with 1¾d of rents; and the homage and service of John le Syre the younger with 1½d of annual rents; and the homage and service of Geoffrey son of Ralph with 1¼d of annual rents; and the homage and service of John Louwyn with 3d of annual rents; and the homage and service of William Toftay with ½d of annual rents; and the homage and service of Geoffrey de Yngling with ½d in annual rents; and the homage and service of William le Warde with a pound of cumin (*cymine*); and the homage and service of John le Syre the elder with 1½d of annual rents, with wardships, reliefs, homages, escheats and all other things which pertain to the said homages with rents, to have and to hold by William, his heirs and assigns, rendering therefrom the due and customary service to the capital lords of the fees. Warranty is granted against all persons in perpetuity. Sealed in witness etc.

[1315 x c.1320]

167. Grant in heredity by William le Warde of Ixworth Thorpe to Thomas of Pakenham, Alice his wife, and Rose their daughter, of a piece of arable land lying in the field of Ixworth Thorpe above his messuage beside the land of Geoffrey son of Ralph on the one side, of which one headland abuts on the grantor's messuage and the other abuts on the land of Thomas, to have and to hold by Thomas, Alice, Rose, and Thomas's heirs and assigns of the capital lord of the fee, rendering to the same the due and customary service. Warranty is granted against all persons in perpetuity. Sealed in witness etc.

[1315 x c.1320]

168. Notification that Bartholomew le Syre has appointed and put in his place William le Syre and John Percy, jointly or severally, to deliver seisin to Thomas,

son of *dominus* William of Pakenham, Alice his wife and William, Thomas's son, of all the lands and tenements which Thomas, Alice and William purchased from the grantor with all appurtenances, as is more fully testified by his charter to Thomas, Alice and William. Sealed in witness etc.

[1315 x c.1320]

169. [*fo. 29v*] Grant in heredity by Bartholomew le Syre of Ixworth Thorpe to Thomas of Pakenham, Alice his wife, and Thomas's son William of two messuages, fifty-six acres of land, two and a half acres of meadow, and 5s worth of rents with appurtenances in Ixworth Thorpe which he purchased from William le Syre his brother and which were formerly of Simon of Gislingham (*Gesselingham*) and Matilda his wife and Richard of Barnham (*Bernham*), with all liberties as in roads, services, meadows, pastures (*pascuis*, *pasturis*), turf-pits, waters, wardships, reliefs, escheats, and all other commodities pertaining to the lands and tenements, to have and to hold all the lands and tenements with all their appurtenances by Thomas and Alice his wife for the whole of their lives of the capital lords of the fees by the due and customary service, and after the death of Thomas and Alice, the lands and tenements with their appurtenances shall pass to Thomas's son William, to have and to hold all the lands and tenements with their appurtenances as is foresaid for the whole of his life of the capital lords of the fees by the due and customary service, and after William's death, all the lands and tenements with their appurtenances as is foresaid shall pass to the rightful heirs of Thomas, to have and to hold all the lands and tenements with their appurtenances as is foresaid of the capital lords of the fees by the due and customary service in perpetuity. Warranty is granted against all persons in perpetuity. Sealed in witness.
Hiis testibus: Petro de Redlygworth, Johanne le Bret, Thoma de Bredewell, Bartholomeo de Lyvermere, Thoma de Berdewell, Willelmo Kenne, Bartholomeo de Okle.

Coney Weston (*Westurn*), Friday 7 Nov. 1315

169a. Grant in heredity by John le Syre of Ixworth Thorpe to Alice, widow of Thomas of Pakenham, and William, Thomas's son, of one piece of land measuring twenty-eight feet in length and three feet in width lying in his messuage at Ixworth Thorpe between his land and that of Alice, that is, abutting at the southern headland on the new ditch of Alice, so that the same boundary between them shall be manifestly and fully fixed, to have and to hold the land with appurtenances by Alice for the whole of her life of the capital lords of the fee by the due and customary service, and after Alice's death, the land shall pass to William son of Thomas, to have and to hold for the whole of his life of the capital lords of the fee by the due and customary service, and after his death, the land with appurtenances shall pass to the rightful heirs of Thomas of Pakenham, to have and to hold of the capital lords of the fee by the due and customary service in perpetuity. Warranty is granted against all persons in perpetuity. Sealed in witness.
Hiis testibus: Willelmo Kenne de Thorp', Thoma Gyle de Saxham, Thoma de

Berdewelle, Thoma Hog de Thorp', Radulfo le Smith, Nicholao le Sire de eadem, et aliis.

Ixworth Thorpe, Thursday 26 April 1330

BL Harleian Charter 56 G 40. Single-sheet original 250mm wide x 110mm; seal, round, approx. 30mm, apparently black wax, though P.D.A. Harvey and A. McGuinness, *A Guide to British Medieval Seals*, London 1996, 17, suggest that 'what appear at first sight to be black seals are nearly always very dark green or brown', sixteen-pointed star, illegible.

170. Agreement between Thomas of Pakenham on the one hand and William Kenne of Ixworth Thorpe on the other, whereby Thomas and William have agreed that they should have and hold all their lands lying in the field called *Northolm* in the vill of Ixworth Thorpe according to an oath taken each year that neither they nor their heirs may have rights of common on each other's lands lying in the said field, unless in manifestly foul weather (*nisi intempere aperto*). Sealed in witness etc.

[1315 x c.1320]

171. Quitclaim by William Kenne of Ixworth Thorpe to Thomas of Pakenham, namely that Thomas and his heirs have the power to enclose and to hold[a] in severalty (*possunt includere et inseperaliter tenere*) a certain meadow called *le Gorehil'* in the vill of Ixworth Thorpe, to have and to hold the meadow in severalty at his will (*pro voluntate sua*), so that neither William nor his heirs nor anyone in their name may henceforth have any right of common or any other right or claim in the meadow, and William [*fo. 30r*] conceded for himself and his heirs to Thomas and his heirs the pasture formerly called *Spenheth* in Ixworth Thorpe to have in severalty with the foresaid meadow for such time as is according to the custom of the vill and the adjacent countryside, and thereafter he or his heirs will restore the common pasture. Sealed in witness.
[b]Hiis testibus: Willelmo de Pakynham, Petro de Redligworth, Bartholomeo de Lyvermere, Henrico Barat, Roberto de le Hil et aliis.

Sapiston 24 June 1315

a Following the 'tenere' in the original BL Harleian Charter 52 D 43, approx. 220mm wide x 95mm, though the cartulary copy has 'retenere'; seal, round, approx. 20mm, natural wax, a running animal, illegible.
b The dating clause and witness list is supplied by the original.

172. Grant in heredity by Nicholas le Syre of Ixworth Thorpe to Thomas son of *dominus* William of Pakenham, kt, and Alice his wife, of a rood of meadow with appurtenances lying in *Sutholm* between the meadow of John le Syre on the one side and that of Thomas on the other, abutting at one headland on the river bank of Ixworth and the other on the herbage of John le Syre, to have and to hold by Thomas and Alice and Thomas's heirs of the capital lord of the fee by the due and customary service, or by whosoever to whom it is granted, sold or assigned in estate by Thomas after Alice's death, freely and quit, in fee and by inheritance.

Warranty is granted against all persons in perpetuity. Sealed in witness, etc., dated etc., year etc.

[1315 x c.1320]

173. Agreement between Thomas of Pakenham on the one hand and William Kenne on the other, when after many controversies they made this concord at the entreaty of their friends, whereby Thomas for himself and his heirs conceded that William and his heirs, from the day on which this agreement was made, may have and possess the whole enclosure surrounding his messuage lying in the vill of Ixworth Thorpe called *le Bekfeld*, in severalty, peaceably, to hold in perpetuity free from challenge or impediment by Thomas or his heirs; and for this concession William in turn conceded for himself and his heirs that Thomas and his heirs may have and possess three enclosures surrounded by Thomas's ditches in the vill of Ixworth Thorpe, of which two are of arable land and the third of meadow fit to be mowed (*falcabilis*) called *le Freth* at *le Springewelle*, in severalty, peaceably, to hold from the day on which this agreement was made in perpetuity free from challenge or impediment from William and his heirs; and William conceded for himself and his heirs that in his foresaid enclosure called *Bekfeld* they shall henceforth not raise or have a fold, and if it should happen that either William or his heirs should raise a fold in the vill of Ixworth Thorpe either inside or outside his enclosure, then they will pay to Thomas and his heirs 20s silver for each night, God forbid that such a fold is erected, on the Sunday immediately after this occurs. Sealed respectively by both parties.

Ixworth Thorpe, Monday 10 June 1319

174. [*fo. 30v*] Agreement in the form of a chirograph between Thomas of Pakenham on the one hand and William Kenne on the other, whereby Thomas conceded and granted in exchange to William a piece of land with appurtenances called *Swynisdich* in the vill of Ixworth Thorpe , to have and to hold by William, his heirs and assigns, freely, quit, well, in fee and inheritance of the capital lords of the fee by the due and customary service. Warranty is granted against all persons in perpetuity. And for this grant William conceded and in exchange granted to Thomas three acres with appurtenances in the vill of Ixworth Thorpe, of which one and a half acres and one rood lie at *Wetelond* between the lands of the said Thomas and one and a half roods lie in the place called *Olde Kennislond*[a] between the lands of Thomas, and one acre lies in two pieces on the quarter called *Banegravewene* between the lands of Thomas, to have and to hold by Thomas, his heirs, and assigns, freely, quit, well, in peace, in fee and by inheritance of the capital lords of the fees by the due and customary service. Warranty is granted against all persons in perpetuity. Sealed respectively by both parties in the form of a chirograph.
Hiis testibus: etc.

Monday 7 Feb. 1317

a over 'Benegnewente'.

175. Quitclaim by William Kenne of Ixworth Thorpe to Thomas of Pakenham of all forms of action, alienation, complaint and demand and to withdraw actions that he has or in anyway might have against Thomas since the beginning of the world until the day on which this was written. Sealed in witness.

Bury St Edmunds (*Sanctum Eadmundum*), Sunday 9 June 1319

Thomas's quitclaim in identical words is preserved as BL Harleian Charter 54 F 2. Single-sheet original 203mm wide x 64mm, tag, seal badly damaged.

176. Grant in heredity by Geoffrey son of Ralph of Ixworth Thorpe to Thomas of Pakenham and Alice his wife, for a certain sum of money in cash, of a piece of arable land lying in the field of Ixworth Thorpe called *Horslond*, whereof one headland abuts on *Chercheweye* and the other on the land of Ralph le Syre, to have and to hold with all appurtenances by Thomas, Alice, and Thomas's heirs and assigns of the capital lord of the fee, freely, quit, well, in peace, in fee and in perpetuity by the due and customary service. Warranty is granted [*fo. 31r*] against all persons in perpetuity. Sealed in witness.
Hiis testibus: etc.

Ixworth Thorpe, Friday 3 Nov. 1318

177. Quitclaim by William son of Geoffrey son of Ralph of Ixworth Thorpe and Sara his sister, for themselves and their heirs, to Thomas of Pakenham and Alice his wife and Thomas's heirs of all right and claim which they had or in anyway might have in a piece of arable land with appurtenances lying in the field of Ixworth Thorpe called *Horsselond*, so that neither William and Sara nor their heirs nor anyone in their name may henceforth have any right or claim therein in perpetuity. Sealed in witness.

Ixworth Thorpe, 1 Nov. 1318

178. Grant in heredity by William le Criketot, kt, to Simon of Gislingham (*Gesselingham*) and Matilda his wife and their heirs, for their service, of an acre of arable land with appurtenances which formerly was of William Sparsus his villein (*rustico*) which Robert son of William returned to the grantor in his court of Ixworth when he was of age, and the said land lies in the field of Ixworth which is called *le Curpetys* between the lands of Simon on both sides, abutting at one headland on the road called *Londesmere*, be there more or less, to have and to hold of the grantor and his heirs by Simon, Matilda his wife, and their heirs or assigns or whosoever to whom they may wish to grant, sell or assign it, freely, quit, well, in peace, in fee and heredity, rendering therefrom annually to the grantor and his heirs 1d of silver at Michaelmas for all services, aids, customs, suits of court and secular demands. Warranty is granted against all persons in perpetuity. Sealed in witness etc.

[March 1269 x 1290]

For a discussion of how the manuscript ends, see pp. 20–1.

INDEX OF PERSONS AND PLACES

In this and the following index, references in roman type are to the charters in this edition; W indicates that the person appears as a witness to a charter. References to the pages of the introduction are in italic type and follow the charter references. The index is arranged by patronymic rather than by Christian name (so Adam, William son of, rather than William son of Adam). Patronymics are listed before occupational descriptions. All places are in Suffolk unless otherwise indicated.

INDEX OF SUBJECTS